D1233547

AIRWAVES TO THE SOUL

The Influence and Growth of Religious Broadcasting

in America

by

Dr. George H. Hill, APR

Published by
R & E PUBLISHERS
P. O. Box 2008
Saratoga, California 95070

Library of Congress Card Catalog Number
81-86007

I.S.B.N.
0-88247-690-4

ABOUT THE AUTHOR

Dr. George H. Hill, APR, communications historian, radio and television producer and journalist, is vice president of Nightingale Communications & Media, instructor of media and public relations classes and director of the Institute of Research. He is accredited by the Public Relations Society of America and holds a Ph.D. in communications. He has graduate degrees in religious information, business administration and humanities, and undergraduate degrees in public relations, education and liberal arts.

A former Air Force captain and squadron commander, his Unity Award winning Ecumenical Insights© radio program focuses on the interfaith and interdenominational aspects of religion in America. "Women In Religion," "Religion My Beat," "The Black Church & Black Spirituality," are some of the innovative specials that received media attention and interest of both the religious and secular communities. Ecumenical Insights© has become the longest airing interfaith radio program in America. Hill produced Year of Sunday, the first Baha'i radio series in Southern California. His involvement in broadcast media began in 1975 when he produced Los Angeles' first black business radio show, Focus on Business. He simultaneously syndicated a newspaper column of the same name that appeared in West and East Coast newspapers. Hill's television experience includes specials telecast on Group W Cable, producer of InterFaith Forum©, the first interreligious program on cable television in Southern California, and associate producer of Get It On in Phoenix, Arizona.

As religion and business writer for the Carson Courier; chairman, Baha'i Media Council and public information officer for the Interreligious Council of Southern California, Hill has been involved in numerous civic, religious and community activities. He has received many awards and citations. These include the California Senate and Assembly; Communicator of the Year, NAMD; Mayor Thomas Bradley and the Los Angeles City Council; Unity Award; Harlem YMCA; Martin Luther King Multiversity; Brotherhood Crusade; Los Angeles County Board of Supervisors; Carson City Council; Boy Scouts of America; National Association of Market Developers' President's Award; and Urban League.

Dr. Hill is a member of the Religious Newswriters Association of North America, Religion In Media, Public Relations Society of America, Black Journalists Association of Southern California, Interreligious Council of Southern California, Baha'i Faith, National Association of Market Developers, YMCA, National MBA Association.

He has also authored *Religious Radio & Television: 1921-1981*, the first annotated bibliography on religious broadcasting; *155 Years of Black Media*, and *Billy Graham: Evangelist Extraordinaire*.

TABLE OF CONTENTS

Page

ABOUT THE AUTHOR iii

PREFACE vii

FOREWORD ix

CHAPTER
   I   Glimpses: Yesterday, Today, Tomorrow 1

   II   Early Pioneers. 5

   III   More Early Pioneers. 10

   IV   Electric Church in Hollywood 18

   V   Black Gospel Trailblazers 30

   VI   Satellite Space Race. 51

   VII   Religious Broadcasting Surveys 64

   VIII   Pay Versus Free Time Religious Broadcasting 85

APPENDIXES
   I   "Religion on the Air in Chicago" by Everett Parker 93
   II   "Who Listens to Religious Broadcasts Anymore?" by
            Ronald Johnstone 107
   III   "Religious Broadcasting in Southern California" by
            George Hill. 116
   IV   "Will Electric Church Replace Traditional Worship?"
            by Emerging Trends 128
   V   "A Telephone Survey of Religious Program Prefer-
            ences Among Listeners and Viewers in Los
            Angeles," by Fred I. Casmir. 130

CHAPTER FOOTNOTES 143

PREFACE

Airwaves to the Soul is a book which describes the growth and influence of religious radio and television in America. The author, Dr. George Hill, has performed a magnificent service by bringing together primary documents and surveys on the theme.

The historical development is well documented.

Since I coined the phrase "The Electric Church" in 1976 I am delighted to see it described in the outset of Chapter I dealing with "Glimpses: Yesterday, Today and Tomorrow." Two chapters bear special mention — namely the "Electric Church in Hollywood" and "Black Gospel Trailblazers," Chapter IV and V respectively. In no other book has there been such a well documented description as contained herein. In fact, these two chapters are worth the price of the entire book.

The Appendix contains the most important documents in the areas of research and surveys and does a great service in bringing this material together in one volume. Undoubtedly, the most controversial and in a way the most interesting chapter is Chapter VIII, "Pros, Cons and Pay, 'Free' Timers." After all, when money is involved people always "sit up and take notice."

I want to commend Dr. George H. Hill for making a most valuable contribution to the ever developing saga of the Electric Church.

Dr. Ben Armstrong
Executive Director
National Religious Broadcasters

FOREWORD

Religious broadcasting, one of the most compelling communications forces of this century, has spread across the world via satellite and shortwave, and across America via AM and FM radio and cable television. Christian broadcasts can be heard in nearly every city and town in this country and in every corner of the globe. And, Jewish, Baha'i and Islamic broadcasts can also air in our living rooms with a flick of the dial.

There was a time when religious programs consisted of little more than a hellfire-and-damnation minister sending the Word of God over bulky, sometimes odd-looking radios. However, today, in addition to much fundamentalist preaching, there are a few dozen gospel music radio stations filling the airwaves with songs of happiness and joy for those who enjoy music.

Religious radio and television has become a business of industrialized proportions. Millions of dollars are spent each year to produce and broadcast the electronic Gospel and has been reclaimed tenfold in the guise of corporate profits and contributions from viewers and listeners. This book traces the roots of religious broadcasting and brings us up-to-date on the subject. But what does the future hold?

Some experts say if current trends are to continue, major Christian denominations will turn en masse toward television preaching as a means to convey their respective messages, a medium which for years has been dominated by individual evangelists. This entry into the field will represent a distinct policy shift by the larger Christian denominations — Roman Catholic, Baptist, Methodist, Mormon — to embrace television as a device of opportunity and seek to enrich its content. Their intent may be to use the medium as a more effective way of accomplishing pastoral work. The Roman Catholic Church and the Southern Baptist Church — the two largest denominations in the United States — are moving toward satellite technology in an effort to establish their own cross-country religious television networks on the order of pioneer Christian networks such as the Christian Broadcasting Network, Praise the Lord Network and the Trinity Broadcasting Network. Besides offering special broadcasts of church-related events and beefed up regular cable network programming, the hookups are destined to be utilized for internal communications and instruction and for the winning of converts. With the deregulation of federal broadcasting guidelines, the advent of more and more local religious radio and television stations is on the horizon.

There is the distinct possibility that all this technology could backfire on church leaders, however. Such technilogical arrangements could reduce the workload of clergymen to the point where the need for such personnel is eliminated. Leaders may also face the death throes of high operating costs and resort to selling advertising to secular interests to keep their operations afloat. Hopefully an equitable balance between technology and reality can be struck so that religion over the airwaves can continue to flourish.

Dr. Hill is to be commended for his diligent research and chronicling of sixty years of religious broadcasting. This book is a valuable tool for seminarians, clergymen, broadcasters, researchers, religion writers and laymen in communications for their examination of the historical aspects of this rapidly growing area of communications.

James C. Kastelic
Religion Editor
Las Vegas Review-Journal

CHAPTER I

GLIMPSES: YESTERDAY, TODAY, TOMORROW

From the time of the radio crystal sets to today's satellite space race by the religious television networks, religious broadcasters have had their sights set on capturing and caressing the souls of listeners via the air waves. This glimpse into historic and demographic realities of religious radio and television may shed some light on the reason why the broadcaster and his audience spend more than $500 million a year.

Little did the Rev. Edwin Van Etten of Pittsburg know when he broadcasted the first religious service on January 2, 1921, from Calvary Episcopal Church over station KDKA, nor was anyone aware when the Radio Church of America in New York began airing the first continuous religious program on November 27, of that same year, that use of the airwaves for religious purposes would be big, big business by 1980.[1] Religious radio and television is seen by many as one of the fastest growing sectors in communications in the 1980's. The 'electric church,' as it usually is called, is indeed one of the true manifested realities of our time. More than 1,400 of the nations 8,000 specialize in religious broadcast, as 30 of the 800 televison stations and 66 of the cable systems, and the number of stations is growing at the rate of one new radio station per week and one new television station per month according to the National Religious Broadcasters Association (NRB).[2]

On October 1, 1951, Norman and Ruth Peale became the first husband and wife team to broadcast a religious program.[3] Now, Paul and Jan Couch, and Jim and Tammy Bakker are on nearly everyday, and Rex and Maude Aimee Humbard are seen frequently.

During his first campaign for the presidency of the United States, Jimmy Carter helped make the words, 'born again' become a household phrase. In 1980, he not only spoke at the NRB convention in Washington,

D.C., he invited religious broadcasters to visit the White House on the following day.[4]

When the itinerant evangelist pitched his tent along the sawdust trail and bellowed his fiery gospel to a few dozen people at best, he was lucky to get enough in his collection plate to get him to the next town. According to *Time Magazine*, there are a half dozen TV ministers who had revenues of $16 to $51 million last year. There are scores of other ministries on television and radio whose broadcasts will take in millions of dollars each year to reach souls via the airwaves.[5]

Cathode Christianity has progressed significantly since 1940 when religious services were first televised on Easter Sunday over NBC station W2XBS.[6] Church services today are telecast via satellite from Israel, Europe and other parts of the world.

It was a big thing for those first services to be televised in New York and Hollywood on the same day. For tomorrow, a consortium of Christian broadcasters are considering the possibility of owning a satellite. By pooling their various resources, they could purchase a 30-channel satellite to broadcast the gospel 24 hours a day, in every major language, to all corners of the globe.[7]

Please decrease the number of programs with a preaching format was a recommendation from the first religious broadcasting survey in 1940. Today, even though there are religious music stations, good interview programs like my show, Ecumenical Insights, and KNBC's Odyssey, and the "Tonite Show" type programs like The 700 Club and PTL (Praise the Lord) Club have come on the scene, religious broadcasting is still overwhelmingly preaching. Hopefully, new technology (cable TV, video disc, etc.) will help to broaden the choices.

During the 1930s and 1940s the Federal Council of Churches of Christ (FCCC), acting as the representative of the Protestant Churches in America, received public service time from the network television stations to broadcast programs. In 1944, the National Association of Evangelicals (the parent organization of the NRB)[8] accused the FCCC of driving paid religious broadcasting off the air because NBC, CBS, and ABC would not sell time to evangelicals. Furthermore, the Mutual Broadcasting System (MBS) which had been selling air time, began limiting commercial religious programs to Sunday mornings, setting a maximum of 30 minutes for individual shows and forbidding direct solicitation of funds over the air. By 1979, however, the tide had turned the other way. Evangelical broadcasters had more time on the airwaves and mainline churches and organizations started losing public service time to groups that would pay for time.[9]

2

Widespread misinformation led to the Federal Communications Commission (the federal agency which licenses and regulates radio and television stations) to receive hundreds of thousands of letters not to ban religious broadcasting—something the agency had never considered doing. The FCC has considered deregulating radio thereby lessening some of the governmental requirements placed on stations. Such a move would mark a revolutionary change in the broadcast industry because it would be the first momentous change since the 1930s. Some religious broadcasters say the change would be good, but mainline church groups have indicated they are not in favor of it.

Another change occurred in May 1980 when the FCC restricted 25 clear channel stations from broadcasting more than 750 miles in any direction. As a result of the ruling, 125 new unlimited time stations have been able to broadcast in local areas at night. A daytime station broadcasting religious programs, after receiving FCC approval, could begin broadcasting 24 hours a day and air many more programs.

The demographics of religious broadcasting was virtually unheard of until recently. Only a handful of surveys have been done over the past 40 years and only two of those were done on a national basis. The research indicates that there has not been much change in the number of persons who watch broadcast "often." Persons of all beliefs and backgrounds watch and listen to religious radio and television much, much more on Sundays than on weekdays. Surveys indicate that people are more tolerant of people of belonging to other religions. In this writer's opinion, broadcasting, with its non-denominational approach and its avoidance of doctrinal matters, has contributed to that increased tolerance. And, it appears that people will be even more tolerant in the future.

Many excellent and exciting religious programs have gone on the air during the past 50 years. It was not until 1977 that the "Emmy" of religious media was established by the Religion In Media Association: the Angel Award. Local and national awards are presented annually for the best religious radio and television programs, films, recordings and forms of media like outdoor advertising. There are expectations that the Angel will become as popular and as coveted as the Emmy and the Oscar awards as America achieves greater spirituality in the future.

DILIGENT VISIONARIES

There were men and women of vision such as Charles Fuller, Lois

Crawford, Walter Maier and dozens of others like them who continued to broadcast through the good and bad times of the early years. They moved us toward today where almost every conceivable religious program is being broadcasted; including music, children's shows, dramas, situation comedies, bible study, news and preaching.

Other men of vision, like William Fore of the National Council of Churches, and Everette Parker, United Church of Christ, have been proponents of excellence, diversity, and research in religious radio and television. People like Pat Robertson, Christian Broadcasting Network; Jim Bakker, Praise The Lord Club; and Ben Armstrong, National Religious Broadcasters, have been influential in promoting and propelling this area of communications around the world.

Twentieth century technology has transformed the old-time, street-corner evangelist into a media personality who is viewed by and listened to by millions. He uses sophisticated camera equipment and satellites to send his message over the airwaves to reach souls.

I have chosen not to include biographical information on the giants of religious broadcasting; such as Billy Graham, Oral Roberts, Robert Schuller or Rex Humbard, because there has been much written about them in other books. Instead I chose to include and bring together information that would be difficult for the reader to find. Additionally, in my annotated bibliography, *Religious Radio & Television, 1921-1981*, there is multitudes of information on the above personalities, the works they have written, the National Association of Religious Broadcasters and ninety percent of the people and organizations that have been involved in religious broadcasting over the past sixty years.

CHAPTER II

EARLY PIONEERS

Sharp forks of lightning flashed across the midsummer night's sky. Window-rattling thunder responded from the banks of black clouds which were an ominous purple and brown by the constant lightning barrage.

Inside a Methodist church in Jackson, Michigan, an evangelist stood before a crude radio microphone, struggling to be heard above the storm. It was his first try at preaching the gospel over the radio.

"As one of the first stations in town," Dr. Clarence Jones said, "WHT was a toy—a gimmick for publicity for the mayor, but to Paul Rader it was God's gift to the unchurched."

An ex-prizefighter, Rader didn't often shy from a new challenge. On June 17, 1922, Rader took a brass quartet, including Clarence Jones (later co-founder of radio station HCJB), up to Mayor Thompson's penthouse radio studio. The studio was an open-air affair with unfinished pinboards put together in sort of a "sentry box" appearance with a hole cut in one side.

"You just get ready and point your instruments at the hole there in the side of the box," a technician instructed the mystified musicians, "and when I say play, you play."

"Play," said a voice, and out of the hole appeared an old telephone microphone. The quartet played and Rader preached. With encouraging listener response from this initial effort, Rader was quick to use other Chicago-area stations — WJJD, WGN, WBBM, WLS — to broadcast the gospel message whenever the chance presented itself over the next five years.

By 1928, network broadcasting had come into its own. NBC was organized into two semi-independent "Red" and "Blue" networks. The Columbia Broadcasting System (CBS) also began operations that year, and by 1930 the "Breakfast Brigade" with Paul Rader and his Tabernacle musicians filled an hour each morning coast-to-coast on CBS.

But that wasn't all of Rader's radio activity. Since WBBM didn't broadcast on Sunday at that time, Rader came up with an idea. He made arrangements with the station and the Federal Radio Commission to use the idle transmitters for 14 hours each Sunday. Call letters WJBT were assigned to the once-a-week station — "Where Jesus Blesses Thousands," Rader said.

The long broadcast was highlighted by two popular evening programs: "The March of the Ages" and the "Back Home Hour." These followed regularly broadcast evening services. According to Dr. Jones, "The March of the Ages," was largely improvised on stage before a live microphone. The other program was not.

"The only idea Rader would give us as staff would be: 'Well, fellows, tonight it's going to be the fall of Jericho.' And with that we'd be thinking of hymns and songs that would suit the theme and narration for the night."

"This was our only training in those days," Dr. Jones continued. "We had plenty of opportunity to try out every idea in the bag."

Despite the increasing use of radio by evangelists and preachers in the early '20s, not all Christians agreed on the worth of radio as a means for reaching lost souls. "It's bound to be a failure as far as the gospel is concerned," some reasoned, "because it operates in the very realm in which Satan is supreme. Is he not the prince of the power of the air?" Others weren't as extreme but felt that radio was a passing fad and that it could only serve to empty churches.

"Paul Rader disproved that idea," Dr. Jones explained. "The Chicago Gospel Tabernacle had a capacity of 5,000 and it was almost always full." The reason? They came to see in person the dedicated men and women they loved to hear on the radio.

Calvary Baptist Church

Other churches jumped into broadcasting. Four months after Rader's first radio experience on WHT in Chicago, a church in New York City realized the possibilities of radio. On October 25, 1922, members of Calvary Baptist Church voted to appropriate $1,000, according to a church bulletin, "to install a radio broadcasting plant to air sermons and music from the church."

Less than five months later, in March, WQAQ, Calvary's own station, went on the air with its evening service. Dr. John Roach Straton delivered the first message over the 250-watt facility. On the occasion of the installation of the broadcasting system in his church a few weeks earlier, Dr. Straton had said, "I shall try to continue to do my part . . . in tearing down the strongholds of Satan, and I hope that our radio system will prove so efficient that when I twist the Devil's tail in New York, his squawk will be heard across the continent."

Despite the small transmitter, WQAQ could be heard over a wide area since only a few stations were broadcasting then. A news item in the New York Evening Mail of April 21, 1923, revealed:

> WQAQ has received reports from receiving stations as far north as Bath, Maine, and as far south as Atlanta, Georgia. Ships have heard it from 500 miles out at sea.

Soon all three Sunday services were being broadcast—at 11 a.m., 3 p.m. and 7:30 p.m.; as was the Wednesday night prayer meetings. In 1927, WQAQ combined with powerful New York station WHN to gain additional outreach.

Though Calvary Baptist no longer owns and operates its own station, the church's radio ministry continues as the country's oldest remaining gospel broadcast. Its broadcasts are now heard on 46 stations in the United States and on powerful overseas stations HCJB, TWR and ELWA.

R. R. Brown

Calvary Baptist isn't the only current broadcast ministry that can date its beginning back to 1923. Just a month after WQAQ went on the air in the East, Dr. R. R. Brown began broadcasting over WOAW (now WOW) in Omaha, Nebraska.

The station itself had only begun broadcasting on April 2, and yet the manager was looking for a minister to preach on WOAW each Sunday. Practically every minister in Omaha had turned down the offer by the time the station official got around to asking Brown, who had been in town less than a year.

Brown agreed to speak on April 8 but was hesitant about accepting the offer to be the station's regular minister. During a service at his Omaha Gospel Tabernacle shortly after the first broadcast, he expressed his doubts about becoming a regular speaker. At the close of the service, a visiting minister — Rev. Newman Hawkins — hurried up to Dr. Brown.

"You'd better be careful," he warned, "Ever since I heard that radio station was being built, I have prayed that God would get an advantage over it."

"If that's the case," Dr. Brown replied, "we had better be careful."

The next morning he called the station to accept the offer to become WOAW's radio pastor. The arrangements were unusual. No contract was ever signed and no salary was ever paid. Dr. Brown's radio service was separate from his regular Sunday services at the Omaha Gospel Tabernacle, since one of the conditions to his acceptance was that his broadcast would be aired before most church services would begin.

On Christmas Day, 1923, Dr. Brown was asked to broadcast a special service to Captain Donald MacMillan and his crew at the South Pole.

By 1925 an estimated 100,000 persons listened each week to Brown's "World Radio Congregation," and he was called the "Billy Sunday of the Air" by a Texas publication. Testimonies from farm families who were prevented from getting to church because of muddy roads and from congregations without pastors who met around the radio for their Sunday morning sermon, indicated to Brown the importance of carrying on such a broadcast.

Until his death in February 1964, the Scotsman from Dagus Mines, Pennsylvania, continued to serve as pastor of Omaha Gospel Tabernacle and WOW. Another Omaha station now broadcasts the program.

Charles E. Fuller

In May 1924 another gospel broadcast inaugurated a lengthy radio ministry. Charles E. Fuller had accepted Christ six years earlier as a result of the preaching of an old classmate from Pomona College (California) — Paul Rader. Shortly after entering the ministry, Fuller went to a Bible conference in Indianapolis. There he substituted for a radio preacher and was profoundly moved by his first experience before a microphone.

"On the train home," Dr. Fuller said, "God spoke to me very definitely about the radio ministry."

Returning home to Placentia, California, he arranged to broadcast his morning and evening services on a 100-watt station in Santa Ana. There weren't many radios in the area in those days. Five or ten letters would have been considered a good listener response. "Our program was very well received, though," Fuller said. "We got 30 letters shortly after we began."

In 1933, he resigned his pastorate in Placentia to devote all of his time to gospel broadcasting, arranging Sunday morning and evening programs on KGER in Long Beach, California. Odds seemed to be against him. On March 10 a disastrous earthquake paralyzed Southern California. When

Fuller arrived at the station for his first broadcast over KGER, nobody was being allowed into the building.

"The police let me in, though, when I told them why I wanted to enter and when they saw the Bible tucked under my arm," Fuller said.

For a time, though, even that seemed to have been a mistake.

"During the broadcast there was an aftershock, and I could see the transmitter swaying back and forth outside the window as I spoke," he recalled. "I said out loud, 'Look out!' There was a volume of mail after that broadcast indicating that many had heard my comment — at least we found out that people were listening."

As if an earthquake wasn't enough, a couple of days later President Roosevelt closed all the banks in the nation, making things difficult for a week-old broadcast dependent on volunteer donations to keep on the air. Yet he was able to make it. His "Pilgrim Hour" on Sunday mornings from 11:00 to 12 a.m., usually attended by about 300, and his evening services, geared primarily to the unsaved, continued from 1933 on KGER over KFI, Los Angeles, and KNX, Hollywood — both 50,000-watt stations.

In 1935, Fuller decided to try an hour broadcast over power KNX, which could be heard in 11 western states, western Canada and Alaska. The day he arrived for his first hour-long program from the huge Hollywood studios, he found a sparse 50 people in the auditorium. For music, he asked for volunteers from the audience, and a 12-voice choir rehearsed quickly for the first hour-long "Old Fashioned Revival Hour."

A management change at KNX in 1937 forced Fuller to switch to a Mutual Broadcasting System hookup on 13 stations, with one as far east as Gary, Indiana. Eight months later a crisis developed. A large corporation wanted Fuller's time spot for a nationwide program.

"Rudy," he told his radio agent, "you let Mutual know that the 'Old Fashioned Revival Hour' will take that network coast-to-coast."

Astonished, the agent asked if he thought he could make it.

"No," Fuller replied, "I cannot, but God can."

So in August 1937, the "Old Fashioned Revival Hour" was heard across the nation on 66 MBS stations. The cost jumped accordingly, from $1,441 to $4,500 a week. The program was on 117 stations by October 1938 and 550 by 1942. A half-hour program since 1958, the "Old Fashioned Revival Hour" — now called "The Joyful Sound" — is heard on more than 143 stations around the world. Though Fuller died in 1968 at the age of 80, the program he founded continues. His son Daniel heads the organization, with David Allan Hubbard doing the speaking.

CHAPTER III

MORE EARLY PIONEERS

Moody Bible Institute

In 1925, two students were playing gospel songs on their cornets and handing out pamphlets at Moody Bible Institute's exhibit at the Illinois Products Exposition. Not far away, Chicago radio station WGES was preparing for a live broadcast from its exhibition. By air time, however, their musicians hadn't shown up. A station official sprinted over to Moody's booth.

"May we borrow your two young musicians?" he asked. Naturally, the boys jumped at the chance to play on the radio.

A few days later the Bible institute received an invitation from WGES to present a one-hour radio program every Sunday at no charge. This taste of what radio could do to spread the gospel whetted the appetites of school officials, who decided to set up a studio and purchase equipment for a station of their own.

On July 28, 1926, WMBI beamed its first broadcast to the residents of Chicago. Since then, the Moody Bible Institute station has pioneered radio drama with a distinctive Christian flavor. It has featured high-quality music and has released many gospel programs. In 1943, FM was added; in 1958 a branch station was erected in Cleveland, and in 1960 another branch station in Moline, Illinois, went on the air. The group of stations is known as the Moody Radio Network.

Donald Grey Barnhouse

One of the first religious broadcasters to go on a nationwide network hookup on a regular basis was Donald Grey Barnhouse. In 1927, he went to pastor the Tenth Presbyterian Church in Philadelphia on one condition that the church change the format of its Sunday evening services to a vespers services, and that the vesper services be broadcast.

From 1928 to 1932, Barnhouse was heard every Sunday evening across the nation on CBS. The vesper service format continued until 1949 when the Philadelphia pastor inaugurated the "Bible Study Hour." Barnhouse began an exhaustive verse-by-verse study of Romans in 1956 that was to take him five years to complete on the study hours. He died in 1961, shortly after he finished the study. James M. Boice is the present speaker on the "Bible Study Hour."

The vaudeville era of radio began in 1930, featuring such notables as Amos 'n Andy, Ed Wynn (the Texaco Firechief), Jack Benny and Bing Crosby. The first year of the depression decade also saw two more gospel broadcasts take the air.

T. Myron Webb

In Texas, Dr. T. Myron Webb began to broadcast health lectures in 1930. A born-again Christian, he went to serve lost souls from the beginning but, according to Mrs. Webb, he tried to bargain with God. "I'll minister to the physical needs of the people," he said, "Someone else can minister to their spiritual needs."

Soon after he began broadcasting his health lectures, Webb recognized the tremendous impact of radio. He decided then to use broadcasting to spread spiritual medicine. On June 26, 1920, he launched a gospel broadcasting ministry that was to span 34 years.

Moving to Enid, Oklahoma, in 1934, Webb started broadcasting a Sunday afternoon Bible class known as "Back to the Bible," on KCRC. Several hundred people began attending the classes and over the years became somewhat of a congregation. They even held their own Wednesday night prayer meetings.

It was in 1934 that a young preacher, Theodore H. Epp, three years out of seminary, met Dr. Webb and was greatly challenged by the potential of radio. The first radio message Epp delivered was on Webb's program in November 1934.

Later, when Webb moved his program to Tulsa to broadcast over KVOO, he changed the name to the "Bible Fellowship Hour." About the same time, Epp was making plans to leave the Southwest to establish a gospel broadcast in Nebraska.

"Since we're changing our name," Webb told him, "you can use our old name — 'Back to the Bible' — if you'd like."

'Lutheran Hour'

In addition to Webb's broadcast, another program was inaugurated in 1930. On October 2, 1930, the late Dr. Walter A. Maier urged listeners of the first "Lutheran Hour" to "cultivate faith built on the sure promises of the Bible, not on hoarded wealth and gilt-edged investments."

To those hearing the broadcast on the 32-station CBS hookup, Dr. Maier's advice cut right to their souls because Americans were seeing first-hand just how fleeting material possessions were. Only a year earlier the stock market had crashed, driving thousands to the brink of despair and suicide.

After 36 weeks, however, "The Lutheran Hour" discontinued because of financial problems and because of a new CBS policy restricting religious programming to Sunday mornings.

But this wasn't the end of the program sponsored by the Lutheran Laymen's league and which was the Missouri Synod of the Lutheran Church. The program was revived on Sunday in 1935. It was given a 13-week trial period over WXYZ, Detroit, and WLW, Cincinnati. Listener response was encouraging, which led officials to sign with the Mutual Broadcasting System for release on an eight-station hookup. Once again Maier was the speaker on October 20, 1935, when "The Lutheran Hour" went on the air to stay from studios at KFUO on the St. Louis Concordia Seminary campus where Maier was a professor.

"The Lutheran Hour" inaugurated overseas broadcasting in English and Spanish over HCJB (Quito) and KXRM (Manila) in 1940. Today "The Lutheran Hour" is released over more than 900 Mutual, NBC and independent stations in the United States and Canada and more than 700 other stations around the world in 41 languages.

The impact of such gospel radio pioneers as Paul Rader and R. R. Brown continued to be felt in the early 1930s as a new venture in broadcasting began to unfold — missionary radio.

Clarence Jones and Reuben Larson

Two men — Dr. Clarence W. Jones and Reuben E. Larson — got the plans rolling that eventually led to the founding of HCJB, Quito, Ecuador.

Dr. Jones had been associated with Paul Rader's gospel radio ministry as a member of the brass quartet that had accompanied the Chicago preacher on his first broadcast on WHT in 1922. Like everyone else in those days, including the "pros," Dr. Jones and the rest of the crew learned by doing.

"In those days," Dr. Jones recalled, "we learned so many things about radio by trying out ideas. Sure, we made mistakes and had many failures, but we always tried to learn from our mistakes and somehow to improve the next time.

"This," he pointed out, "was great training for the mission field radio work. Through those years of training God was getting me ready for something else — something about which I hadn't the slightest idea then."

Reuben Larson was Jones' co-visionary and, like Jones, he was influenced greatly by one of the first radio preachers — Dr. R. R. Brown of Omaha, Nebraska. After his graduation from St. Paul (Minn.) Bible Institute, Larson became engaged in itinerant evangelism and pastoral work, while keeping an eye on mission field possibilities. One day, while attending a conference in a Duluth, Minnesota church, he had the opportunity to hear Brown speak.

Larson was moved by the radio pastor's enthusiastic account of the opportunities to preach the gospel over the airwaves. He decided that if he was ever given the chance, he, too, would accept the challenge to use the airwaves to win souls for Christ. It was not long after that that Reuben Larson met with Jones in Chicago.

There they discovered they shared many similar ideas on missionary radio broadcasting. Soon Larson and his wife were on their way to the mission fields of Ecuador, taking with them plans and ideas for a radio station in South America.

On August 15, 1930, Larson secured a broadcasting license from the Ecuadorian government for what would be the first radio station in the entire country. But he needed more than just a license — a transmitter and engineer, for example. And God provided.

CBS had assigned a young engineer, Eric Williams, to work the "Breakfast Brigade" program, which originated from the Chicago Gospel Tabernacle each morning. Listening to the gospel day after day, he soon became convinced of his need for the Lord. Eventually, he was led to Christ by Clarence Jones.

As he became aware of the plans for a missionary radio station, he quit his job with CBS to devote his time and talent to designing and building a 200-watt transmitter. Williams became the station's engineer on

Christmas Day, 1931, when HCJB — "The Voice of the Andes" — went on the air for the first time. A new era had begun.

Clarence Erickson

But another era ended two years later when, in 1933, Clarence Erickson accepted Paul Rader's invitation to take over the ministry at the Chicago Gospel Tabernacle. Erickson also took over Rader's daily radio program which was being broadcast by WLS.

Within a few months, Erickson switched his broadcast to WCBD in Waukegan, traveling 75 miles round trip from Chicago each morning for him and his organist, Merrill Dunlop, a veteran of Rader's radio days. This was the beginning of the "Heaven and Home Hour."

When WCBD changed its call letters to WAIT and moved to Chicago, Erickson and the "Heaven and Home Hour" went along. In 1941, Des Moines radio station WHO was added and a network was gradually built up. Today the program's headquarters are in Glendale, California, and the ministry is directed by Erickson's successor, Russell Killman.

Several other gospel broadcasts were spawned in the 1930's, possibly as a reflex action to meet the needs of a nation discouraged by economic depression and severe drought. Besides Erickson's "Heaven and Home Hour," there were Paul Meyers' "Haven of Rest" and J. Harold Smith's "Radio Bible Hour."

Paul Meyers

Paul Meyers rose to the position of executive manager of two Southern California radio stations before drinking cost him his job. After overcoming alcoholism, Meyers felt God's call to the ministry, but his only training was in broadcasting. Using the abilities God had given him, Paul Meyers — or "First Mate Bob," as he was known on the program — soon developed the "Haven of Rest" format, featuring quartet and organ music with short evengelistic messages. The first program was released in March 1934.

J. Harold Smith

J. Harold Smith's "Radio Bible Hour" was another mid-Depression entry into gospel broadcasting that survived. The program has been on the air continuously since the first broadcast on December 1, 1935.

Like the other pioneers in gospel radio, Smith had a conviction that such a broadcast was the will of God. This gave him the necessary faith to pay in advance for the first program. He recalls the incident:

> "In December of 1935, I walked into a radio station in Greenville, South Carolina, and asked if they would sell me time for a daily program. The manager, hoping to scare me off, I think, said, 'Yes, but you'll have to pay $100 a week for the first five programs — in advance.'"

From his total assets of $110, he paid the station manager the requested amount, leaving himself a $10 bill. Yet on the Monday afternoon of the second week he was able to walk in with a second $100 to pay for his next five broadcasts.

John Zoller

The year 1938 was not a good one for the human race in general. Ominous war clouds were gathering over Europe. War seemed inevitable.

But that was also the first year for John Zoller's "America Back to God Hour." Zoller, whose gospel radio experience dated back to the 1922 Methodist revival meeting in Michigan, had been active in broadcasting throughout the '30s. By 1935 he had daily programs on Detroit's WMBC and WEXI, as well as on stations in New York City, Baltimore, Chicago and others. Then, as global events seemed sure to draw the United States into war, Zoller was asked to gear his gospel broadcasts to America's servicemen.

"During the war," Zoller said, "the 'America Back to God Hour' could be heard over stations on every continent, on War Department stations as well as Mutual network stations and independents in this country until 1946."

Since then, Zoller has continued a limited radio ministry in addition to literature and tract distribution.

M. R. De Haan

The "Radio Bible Class' is one of the most beloved programs of all time. It also began in 1938. Leaving a medical practice a few years after receiving his M.D. from the University of Illinois, M. R. De Haan returned to school, this time to Western Theological Seminary in Grand Rapids, Michigan. After a short pastorate in his denomination following graduation, De Haan left to establish an independent congregation at a theater in Grand Rapids. (Theaters were closed on Sundays in that city.)

His Bible teaching became well known, and soon he found himself conducting weekly Bible classes in Flint, Buffalo and Detroit. The classes were in addition to his responsibilities at his own church. As a result of the Friday and Saturday Bible classes in Detroit, De Haan began his "Radio Bible Class" over a small Detroit-area station. Today the half-hour Bible-study program is heard on nearly 500 stations each week. Richard De Haan, who had begun working for his father in the shipping room at the age of 16 and, by his own admission, had worked in "about every other department in the place," took over the speaking chores of the "Radio Bible Class" upon the death of his father in December 1965.

Two more gospel programs entered the broadcasting arena before the end of the decade: "Back to the Bible Broadcast" and the "Back to God Hour."

Theordore Epp

Early in April 1939, a young preacher from Oklahoma nervously waited to be called into the office of the managers of two jointly owned stations in Lincoln, Nebraska. As a matter of fact, Theodore H. Epp said, "To be quite frank, I was very much afraid."

But God was at his side, just as He had stood by other courageous men who had dared to believe that radio could be used to bring souls to Christ.

"We note that you have everything on your broadcasts that people want except something from the heart," Mr. Epp boldly told the station managers. "We have that and would like the opportunity of presenting it to the people."

The managers, evidently impressed with the applicant's sincerity and realizing that a gospel program might be what their stations needed, expressed a willingness to take on the program.

"I asked to purchase a 30-minute daily period on the larger of the two stations — 10,000-watt KFAB," he explained. "But instead, a few days later, I was offered a contract for 15 minutes on the 250-watt KFOR at $4.50 per program."

So on May 1, 1939, the "Back to the Bible Broadcast" (Mr. Epp had decided to accept T. Myron Webb's offer of the use of the name) was heard for the first time on the small local station. First station additions to "Back to the Bible's" network came in 1941 when WNAX, Yankton, South Dakota, and then SMA, Shenandoah, Iowa, and KVOD, Denver, Colorado, were added. By the end of 1942, five more stations had been added to the network. In 1943 powerful HCJB beamed "Back to the Bible" internationally for the first time. At the end of the year the broadcast was being released 102 times a week. Today, "Back to the Bible" is released on more than 500 stations around the world, most of which release the program six times a week — a total of more than 3,800 releases a week.

Harry Schultze

The "Back to God Hour," the radio ministry of the Christian Reformed Church, also began in 1939. As much as 10 years earlier the denomination had recognized the need for a radio voice, but it wasn't until 1938 that a radio committee was appointed.

Then the wheels started moving and in less than a year — on December 17, 1939 — the first "Back to God Hour" was released over WJJD, Chicago, with the late Dr. Harry Schultze as speaker.

In 1940 the program was expanded to a 26-week season for nine seasons and to a year-round schedule by 1943. December 7, 1947 marked the first broadcast over Mutual network, which continues to release the "Back to God Hour" for a half hour each Sunday. Dr. Peter Eldersveld took over the speaking chores in 1946 and was its voice until his death in 1965.

CHAPTER IV

ELECTRIC CHURCH IN HOLLYWOOD

Southern California, the home of the stars, Hollywood and big cars, is said to have more religious programs and stations than any other region in the world. The yellow pages in the city of Los Angeles lists 13 full pages of churches; everything from African Methodist Episcopal to Vedanta Society. Additionally, there are 205 groups listed as religious organizations in a separate category of the yellow pages. There are separate phone books for ten other clusters of cities in Los Angeles County which list even more church and religious organizations.

One organization that is representative of the major world faiths in the area is the Interreligious Council of Southern California (IRC). This is the most diverse interfaith body in the nation and perhaps in the world because it has as members; Baha'is, Buddhists, Catholics, Greek Orthodox, Jews, Moslems, Protestants, Sikhs and Vedanta.

Consequently, it is easy to see that Southern California also contains more religious programming than any geographical region in America.

There are 13 AM and FM radio stations and two television stations that are designated as religious stations and, according to the National Religious Broadcasters Association's (NRB) Directory of Religious Broadcasting, there are 30 Southern California based companies producing religious programming. Moreover, when including the network, independent, public broadcasting, cable and noncommercial stations, religious oriented programs are phenomenal in number. For example, on Sunday television with two religious stations, (KHOF and KTBN) and the 13 secular television stations, one can watch television from 5:00 a.m. until midnight and have a choice of three completely different religious programs.

The First Station

Radio station 6ADA (later KNX) was the first radio station to begin broadcasting in Los Angeles on September 10, 1920.[1] A man named Christian — Fred Christian — opened up the airwaves in Southern California. During the early 1920's, people bought their parts and built their own radios. The Department of Commerce, then the broadcasting regulatory agency, had all the Los Angeles stations broadcasting over 360 meters. By the summer of 1922, more than 20 other stations in and around Los Angeles had also been licensed to broadcast. With all the stations sharing a single wavelength of 360 meters, the rivalry between the operators of the stations became quite intense. However, Fred Christian survived. Out of this chaos in early broadcasting around the Los Angeles area, there emerged only three stations still broadcasting today; KNX (1920), KHJ (1922) and KFI (1922).[2]

No one seems to know for sure which stations, if any, had a religious broadcast between 1920 and 1923. But some old timers suggest that there must have been a few because the news must have traveled west about the first religious broadcast in the United States, which occurred on January 2, 1921, in Pittsburg, Pennsylvania.

Sister Aimee Starts KFSG

Aimee Semple McPherson, founder of Angelus Temple in Los Angeles, had a flair for communicating. Soon she translated her talent electronically through radio by establishing the first religious radio station in Los Angeles.

She explains in her book, *Story of My Life*:

Then came the challenge of radio! There were only two stations in Los Angeles in 1923. When I sat before my receiving set, over came floating to my ears songs, music recitations, as clearly and distinctly as though instruments were playing and voices singing right in the room. And yet they were being broadcast miles away. My soul was thrilled with the possibilities this media offered for the spread of the gospel. We secured time on a radio station and began broadcasting services. But the thought persisted that if Angelus Temple had her own radio station, we could broadcast all meetings! In February, 1924, KFSG-Kall Four Square Gospel went on the air.

19

During the depression, McPherson sold the daytime hours of KFSG to Los Angeles attorney Frank Dothery so that she could obtain money to repay loans and feed the hungry. Several years later, he obtained permission from the FCC to use the call letters KRKD-AM to operate on the same frequency with KFSG. In 1947, Dothery acquired station KRKD-FM and in 1950, sold KRKD-AM to Transamerica Broadcasting. Transamerica's owner died in 1960 and the estate was settled when the International Church of the Foursquare Gospel bought back the daytime station KRKD-AM. Both night-time and daytime KRKD were reunited again operating around the clock as KRKD-AM and FM. The stations broadcasted 30 percent religion and 70 percent beautiful album music.

"We were either fish or fowl with the religion and beautiful music format," explains Charles Duarte, executive secretary, International Church of the Four Square Gospel, "and, we were having difficulties getting advertisers and several other problems."

In 1970 the FM station became automated and KRKD-AM was sold to a station now known as KIIS. The FM station was again assigned to call letters KFSG. And, according to Duarte, KFSG-FM became the first station in the nation to go with primarily all gospel music format. "We broadcast 10 to 20 minutes of inspirational messages each hour, but the majority of the time it is beautiful gospel music. This gives the listener time to think about the message the speaker has given. We do not think people want to be preached to death, "That's why our format is mostly music."

While Sister Aimee was strengthening her KFSG broadcast in Los Angeles, KPPC in Pasadena began broadcasting on Christmas Day in 1924 at Pasadena Presbyterian Church. At 8 a.m., a switch was pulled to present a live program of Christmas carols followed by a morning Christmas service. The next Sunday, both morning and evening services were broadcast.

The church started the station at the urging of Frank Thorne, a young layman crippled with arthritis. He encouraged the pastor, Dr. Robert Freeman, to start a station by giving the first gift for it.

The Pasadena church operated on a non-commercial basis until 1973, when Universal Broadcasting Corporation purchased KPPC.[3] Now a commercial religious station, KPPC has continued to carry the Pasadena Presbyterian Church worship service on Sunday mornings, making it one of the longest running religious programs on the air. Another thing that makes KPPC an unusual station is its schedule. Most stations broadcast every day. But KPPC is licensed to operate only on Sunday and on Wednesday evenings, 22½ hours a week with 100-watts power. When it is on the air, certain nearby stations are required to reduce their power to prevent interference.

KPPC's sister station, KMAX-FM, is housed in the same building and owned by Universal. It also has a religious format. "It is geared to a black and foreign language audience," said Darby Cunningham, KMAX general manager. Ollie Collins, Los Angeles' top disc jockey and gospel concert promoter, says that the station has become a favorite of black listeners, because it airs contemporary gospel music and top black gospel artists such as Andrae Crouch, Danibelle, Walter Hawkins and James Cleveland, to name a few.

First Religious TV Station

KHOF-FM and KHOF-TV (Channel 30) are part of the Faith Broadcasting Network Headed by Pastor Gene Scott of Faith Center Church in Glendale. The church also owns WHCT (Channel 18) in Hartford and KVOF (Channel 38) in San Francisco. According to Scott, KHOF-TV is the oldest, exclusively religious television station in the United States. It entered the Christian television field in 1969. (At this time CBN was telecasting large portions of secular programming in addition to their religious format. CBN's first station in Virginia was the second religiously-oriented station.) According to Joe Shackleford, KHOF-TV operations engineer, KHOF was also the first religious station in the country to telecast 24 hours a day.

Each evening at 7 p.m., Pacific time, the four entities of Faith Center Church air Scott's "Festival of Faith." In California, Channel 30, Channel 38 and KHOF-FM participate in a three-station microwaved simulcast. (The Connecticut station telecasts "Festival" by tape-delay.) Scott says that it is the only regular simulcast, either on commercial or religious stations, of its kind.

"Festival" has both singing and bible teaching. Scott leads discussion about the role of the church in modern society and asks viewers and listeners to apply Christ's teachings and principles in their everyday lives. Scott believes there is a lack of respect in the secular field today for religious institutions; consequently, he challenges labor boards, tax officials, communications agencies, and any group or entity which encroaches on what he feels are "the constitutionally guaranteed rights of his church." Scott's ministry is truly unique, so much so that persons in the secular media do not know what to say of him and his Faith Center Church. The San Francisco Chronicle called Scott a "Johnny Carson-for-Jesus." However, media has also dubbed Pat Robertson of CBN's 700 Club, and Bakker of PTL with the same title. Additionally, the Chronicle also said that Scott is a "phenomenal success" at fund raising and appears to "thoroughly relish" legal battles involving church rights. He was characterized by New West Magazine as ". . .fighting a desperate battle against the devil on his right and the tax man on his left."[4]

Born Again Radio — KYMS, KBRT

In recent years, several newcomers have made their way into the "born again" radio market in Southern California. "Championing the straight approach" by sticking strictly with up-tempo, contemporary Christian music is KYMS-FM, which first aired its format six years ago from Santa Ana. General manager, Arnie McClatchey, shoots for an 18 to 34 year old listener. Geared to the same audience is KBRT-AM, sister to Los Angeles' top-rated KBIG-FM, the "beautiful music" outlet. KBRT plays a mixture of up-tempo contemporary Christian music, and well-screened "middle of the road" (MOR) music and pop. Though based in Los Angeles, KBRT's signal is beamed 26 miles across salt water from Santa Catalina Island, resulting in an amplification of its signal to Orange County — KYMS' exclusive turf until KBRT's debut two years ago.

Prior to KBRT's debut, McClatchey stuck to typical on-air promotions, relying on giveaway trips, etc., to attract listeners. But now he does remotes once a month from four contemporary Christian bookstores; one each weekend per month, with T-shirts, posters and other prizes. McClatchey also broadcasts weekly contemporary Christian concerts from a local chapel, which has asked him to keep the crowd (now at 5,000 persons) trimmed down.[5]

KYMS-FM broadcasts six hours of Bible instruction every day until noon, after which the music begins and lasts the rest of the day. Except for the instructional portion, McClatchey insists, "a listener couldn't tell we were a religious station."

"We're trying to make it an adult contemporary station that really reaches that vast spread of 18-49 year-old persons without being offensive to anybody." says McClatchey, a 20-year veteran of secular radio who has guided KYMS since its rebirth as a Christian station.[6]

The key to success with a commercially operated music format is spot sales. Probably no other factor has hindered the growth of contemporary Christian music stations more because the concept is still so new for Christian radio. In earlier days almost all of the advertisers on KYMS were Christian businesses, but that alone did not spell success.

"It became apparent very quickly that we could develop regular advertising revenues from the agency business world," said McClatchey, adding that the agencies are finally becoming receptive to the idea of buying spots on KYMS. The reason is ratings.

"Our ratings are very good compared to other Christian radio stations, and they are very, very good compared to our secular counterparts. We've even beaten some of our local AM stations in certain periods," says McClatchey (KYMS does not subscribe to a rating service.) "However, we are starting to get some business from agency people because they know that we have been around now for six years and we are gaining a large audience and we are reaching a responsive and loyal audience. Advertisers are looking every day for new ways to get their products out and for new avenues to reach more people. We tell them that if they are going to buy radio, they should include KYMS as part of that radio buy because we are reaching people they can't reach with other stations."[7]

KBRT, a daytime AM station, is making its mark in the marketplace and Ed Lubin, KBRT's sales manager, speaks along the same lines as McClatchey.

"You listen to my radio station and you can't tell the difference. It's not 'Jesus Loves You;' we're playing B. J. Thomas, Pat Boone and Debbie Boone,"[8] Lubin said.

The impact of KBRT-AM, presented as "The Bright Life," has been extraordinary according to Jack Adamson, KBRT general manager.

"We can't keep up with the mail and the phone never stops ringing. We seem to have found a need that we can fill, that being inspirational radio or 'born again radio' as many Los Angelinos prefer to call it, said Adamson.

However, Adamson is not fond of the born again label; he suggests that the phrase "inspirational radio" is more appropriate.

Prior to coming to KBRT, Adamson discussed the Debbie Boone hit song, "You Light Up My Life," with associates. He discovered it was called a "cross-over" tune, meaning a pop recording that had gained acceptance on the religious music stations. Adamson says that he didn't understand why "cross-overs" don't happen more often; consequently, he knew that an inspirational format could work for KBRT.

The KBRT format consists of three contemporary Christian or inspirational songs followed by one Top 40 tune, all with an upbeat tempo. No gospel or heavily religious numbers are included, nor does the station accept any religious advertising. Adamson says that his station is offering listeners music with a rock beat while featuring a Christian message. "We are looking for the young people who grew up with rock music and are now looking for something more in their lives."[9]

"Young people today don't want to be preached at," said Adamson. "They can make up their own minds."

Whether it's called inspirational radio, 'born again' radio or that ole time religion programming, contemporary religious radio is picking up listeners and helping to sell more gospel records than ever before.

Fulfilling Needs

KTYM, owned by Transamerican Broadcasting, attempts to fill the needs of many ethnic communities.

"We broadcast 16 black ministers of various denominations each week," says Robert Hardyway, the station's program director. "Our foreign language programs include Japanese Protestant, Italian Catholic, German Methodist, Remanian Baptist and Russian Prtestant."

Gererdo Borrego, KTYM's general manager, says that his station also airs non-religious foreign programs, and is one of a few stations in the country that deals with a wide variety of ethnic programs. Borrego adds that most of the evangelical ministers on KTYM are Pentecostal and Church of God. There are also a small percentage of Baptists and other denominations, he said.

A daytime station at 1460 on the dial, KTYM plays gospel music at the end of its weekday broadcast. The Rev. Raymond Branch, KTYM disc jockey, mans that time slot with the "Rainbow Gospel Hour." He says that over the past 13 years the black audience has increased 150 percent because there is not another station in Los Angeles which broadcast gospel music during afternoon drive time.

Successful Format

KGER, a station which broadcasts mostly preaching programs, has not changed its format since 1949. It broadcasts 24 hours a day, 7 days a week and can be heard as far away as San Diego.

Because of its pioneer regional status dating back to 1926 and its seniority at the 1390 spot on the dial, KGER is one of the few stations that is not required to reduce its power at twilight.

"We're one of a few religious stations which shows up on national surveys," says Clinton Flower, general manager since 1951, "and for that, you need a minimum one percent of the listeners at any hour, day or night. That is, for us, 75,000 to 100,000 at any time listening frequency. That is a minimum. We calculate there are several hundred thousand who listen frequently — and many more occasionally."

KGER has 75 major accounts, most of them for more than 30 years, which would seem to be an index of satisfaction with listenership. The station also airs many public service programs in addition to preaching. A prominent example of non-religious community service is the fact that since 1928 KGER has donated 9,000 broadcasting hours to the Long Beach Municipal Band, an estimated $750,000 worth of time.

The station's basic thrust was established by its founder, John Brown of Arkansas, who was converted to Christianity through the Salvation Army but never professed a denomination. The Christian university which bears his name in Siloam Springs, Arkansas, is the parent organization of the radio operation.[10]

When asked about the effect that contemporary religious music stations have had on KGER, Jay Davis, program director, says, "There is very little effect; you must realize that our format has been successful for 30 years. Why should we change? We believe that we have our audience, and other stations may appeal to a different demographic market."

Infinite Variety

You asked for it and you got it in Los Angeles, XPRS, a Mexican station broadcasts religious programs from 6:30 p.m. until midnight and airs mostly Eastern-based preachers, such as Reverend Ike. XPRS has been broadcasting for nearly five years. Its predecessor on the same frequency, XERB, also offered religious programming. The station airs programs in Spanish for a Hispanic audience during daytime hours.

One of Long Beach's contributions to religious broadcasting has been KFRN, the only non-commercial religious station in Southern California. Station Manager, Fred Whiteman, said that it is illegal for the station to sell time and it is not allowed to broadcast advertisements. It is operated strictly on contributions from listeners. KFRN began broadcasting in November 1977, and is a 24 hour station.

"More than half of our programming is contemporary Christian music," says Whiteman, "But we do a fairly extensive amount of public affairs."[11] KFRN is one of nine stations owned and operated by Family Stations, Inc., in Oakland, California.

The newest station in the market as of December, 1979, is KIIS-AM, calling itself "1150 AM—the radio voice of Inspiration." It is the sister station to KIIS-FM, a Southland disco favorite. Both stations are owned by communications conglomerate, Combined Communications Corporation.

When asked why KIIS-AM went religious in a market where there were already 12 religious stations, station manager and controller, Rusty Faust, laughingly, but sternly, replies, "We felt we could be competitive in the marketplace because we have a strong signal covering a wide area with a population of over 11 million people."

The station's signal covers seven countries. It can be heard from Bakersfield to San Diego and Riverside to Santa Barbara. "Consequently, an advertiser buying time on the station can reach a lot more listeners," adds Faust.

The station is formatted as MOR (middle of the road) for a 34-years-old-plus age group. According to Faust the station has Jewish programs as well as Christian music, preaching ai d public affairs. The same disc jockeys who worked at the station before it went religious are still there and enjoying it.

Jewish Perspective

The Jewish community in Southern California has broadcast a variety of programs on radio and television over the years. Israel Today Radio, produced by Phil Blazer and the Israel Today Media Group, has been on KUTE for 14 years. It is the longest running Jewish program broadcast in the Los Angeles area. The program, currently airing from 9-11 a.m. Sundays, consists of Jewish-Israeli music, local news, national and international news.

Israel Today Television telecasts a half hour on Sundays, on KSCI, Channel 18. Like Israel Today Radio, it is primarily a news program. The television program also airs in New York City and New Jersey.

Since 1971, Rabbi Max Vorspan has been hosting 'Commitment,' a half hour talk show on KNXT-TV, Channel 2. "The uniqueness of our program," says producer Thelma Post, "is our willingness to take risks and deal with the issues of the day. We discuss news items, interfaith, ethnic, and cultural topics, as well as Jewish topics." The program telecasts 13 to 20 weeks a year.

"Rap With Rabbi Mike" on KABC-TV was telecast from 1972 to 1974. Hosted by Mike Menitoff, the 13 week series dealt with a variety of topics of interest to the community. Menitoff also hosted 'Jewish Response to Youth' which aired for eight weeks in 1976 on KABC-TV. The focus of the program centered around the interest of teenagers; i.e., education, drugs, sports, and dating. This was the first program in Los Angeles that was oriented toward Jewish youth, according to Menitoff.

The American-Israeli Jewish Hour, hosted by Linda Tallen, airs Sundays on KWHY, Channel 22.

Other radio programs include "Jewish Federation Presents" on KFAC and the Union of American Hebrew Congregations which has a 15-minute broadcast on Sunday mornings on KGIL.

Ecumenical Insights Is Interfaith

Although Southern California has a choice variety of Christian broadcasts, some Jewish programs are occasionally about other world faiths. There have been only two programs which have continuously dealt with those organizations, topics, people and events which are brining the world's great religions together — an exclusively interfaith and interdenominational format. These shows were produced by my company, Nightingale Communications and Media.

The first one is "Ecumenical Insights" on KSUL. According to articles in the *Long Beach Press Telegram, South Bay Daily Breeze* and the *Carson Courier*, this program has received awards for broadcasting, unity and togetherness among religions. The broadcast is a half hour interview talk show. However, some programs have included music to express and share feelings. Ecumenical Insights has aired unique specials on topics never dealt with before by other programs in Southern California or America. These specials include: "Women in Religion," "The Black Church and Black Spirituality," "The Interreligious Council of Southern California," and "Religion My Beat." There are future specials being scheduled on contemporary religious music, academic religion, Negro spirituals and religious books.[12]

InterFaith Forum, a series of television programs primarily telecast over cable stations and one network station, has aired programs which spiritually blend mankind and discuss the samenesses among religions. It is a half hour talk show, some of which have been about the National Conference of Christians and News, Academy of Judaic, Christian, and Islamic Studies, Los Angeles Council of Churches, Southern California Council of Churches, Baha'i Faith and others.[13]

Network Affiliates

With 80 radio stations in the Los Angeles market, there are more religious programs than one can count. Television is a bit more definitive because programs are usually listed in the *TV Guide*. The network affiliate stations telecast weekly religious programs. KABC's "Dimensions" on Channel 7 is hosted by Mary Dorr who is also the Executive Director of Religion in Media. KNXT, Channel 2, telecast "Today's Religion" KNBC, Channel 4, is the only station which chooses to have a full-time staff person whose only job is to produce the station's religious program. Beth MacKenzie is producer of KNBC's "Odyssey."

Religion In Media

Southern California is the home of Religion in Media Association (RIM), a non-profit organization supported by donations of groups, denominations and individuals who are interested in top quality religious-oriented material in the media. RIM acts as liaison between the various religious communities and the media industry. It is involved in producing, promoting, coordinating and distributing television and radio programs of moral and spiritual value for presentation on public service time.

Part of the real uniqueness of RIM, which makes it unlike any similar organization, is that broadcasters provide public service time to religious organizations through RIM. In a major market like Los Angeles, scores of religious groups are requesting and competing for public service time. In the early 1970's, several broadcasters turned to RIM to serve as a clearing house and coordinator for these requests, and to produce quality programs which could be used by their stations.

Mary Door, RIM's executive director, says that RIM produces 500 original programs per year, distributes 463 programs during an average month, and coordinates an excess of 3,000 hours of TV and radio programming every 12 months. Public service time is donated by independent network stations for RIM productions or programs distributed by RIM, which, in the past two years, has had an annual market value of $53 million. In 1977, RIM held its first award banquet honoring exceptionally well-written and skillfully produced religiously-oriented material in motion pictures, television, radio, press and other media. The purpose of the RIM Awards programs is to honor media which contribute to the continued moral heritage of America and to reward persons that have produced uplifting and spiritually refreshing material. The award, which is called an "Angel," is presented for national and local quality productions in ten categories.

Baha'i Programs

Baha'i radio series have received good response from listeners. According to the Baha'i National Information Office in Wilmette, Illinois, "Baha'i Perspectives: The Jeff Reynolds Show" has aired on several Southern California stations and on 300 other stations throughout the United States. A very entertaining series of 16 programs, Reynolds shares Baha'i principles, such as the oneness of God, oneness of religion, and oneness of humanity and intersperses them with Top 40 hits by Elton John, Stevie Wonder, England Dan and John Ford Coley, and Gladys Knight and the Pips.

"Year of Sunday," a weekly talk show on KSUL focuses on unity in diversity of religion with a variety of Baha'is sharing their thoughts on religion, why they became Baha'is, and why the Baha'i Faith is not just a religion to them but a way of life. Guests have included Dizzy Gillespie, Parker McGee, Stu Gilliam, Fayard Nicholas of the Nicholas Brothers, Seals and Crofts, and U. S. District Judge Dr. Dorothy Nelson.[14]

CHAPTER V

BLACK GOSPEL TRAILBLAZERS

They shout! They sing! And, oh boy, do they preach! But just as in secular broadcasting, only a minute handful of blacks have broken through the barriers to be continuously seen on television. So it is in religious broadcasting. Only a few blacks have had continuously telecast programs. Scores of black churches in a variety of major cities have been on television once or twice. There are black ministers and churches who have been on television in their local areas from five to 15 years. However, only four black ministers and one black layman have telecasts that are currently being viewed in ten or more states. They are: Reverend Ike of New York, Reverend Clay Evans of Chicago, Reverend Fred Price, located in Inglewood, California, a suburb of Los Angeles, and Reverend Cleophus Robinson of St. Louis. Ben Kinchlow of the Christian Broadcast Network's 700 Club has probably received more national television exposure than any other black in religious television.

Reverend Ike

More than 15 years ago, Frederick J. Eikerenkoetter II, better known as Reverend Ike, was a poor black fundamentalist preacher with a storefront church, hardly able to pay his rent and buy food. However, today there has been more written about Ike and his ministry than any other black minister in America.

In 1965, Reverend Ike decided that he should leave the hellfire and damnation preaching and began to espouse, "If you want pie in the sky by and by when you die, then Reverend Ike is not your guy," and adding, "You can have it here and now and with a cherry on top."

He is one of the most widely heard radio preachers. Ike's sermons are heard on 85 radio stations each week with either 15 or 30 minute programs, ranging from daily to weekly broadcasts. His crusades have been conducted only in the United States in 30 states, but more than 1500 radio broadcasts are heard each month in Mexico, Canada and the Caribbean.[1] He also videotapes his services which are shown on television stations across the nation at later dates. And, from time to time, he has presented regional television specials which have been seen by millions. He produces two publications: a bi-monthly magazine called *Action* and a quarterly called *Science of Living Study Guide*. These magazines are mailed to more than 1.5 million of his followers. It has been reported that he draws more people to his meetings than any other evangelist (with the exception of Billy Graham). Unquestionably, Reverend Ike has one of the largest congregations in the United States. Born the son of a Baptist preacher, and a native of Ridgeland, South Carolina, with ancestors going back to the Dutch Caribbean, Ike knew extreme poverty in his youth. He recalls for his audience the times when he walked barefoot to a one-room school, where his mother was the only teacher. In 1956 he received a bachelor of theology degree from the American Bible College in Chicago. He founded the United Church of Jesus Christ for All People in Ridgeland, after serving two years as an Air Force chaplain. In 1964, he moved out of the South and into Boston where he established the Miracle Temple. Though his mammoth mail ministry (nearly 2 million letters pour in monthly, and each donor has his own little niche in the computers) is still Boston-based, Ike found New York better suited for his church. After moving to Manhattan, Ike left his old-time religion for his "new-time science of living."

Ike is pastor of the United Church in the Washington Heights section of Manhattan. His church has grown so rapidly that it now has several associate ministers to help provide spiritual leadership. Although Reverend Ike's United Evangelistic Association receives financial support from many whites in his very large radio audience, the members of his 5,000 seat sanctuary are predominantly black. The people who come to hear him week after week are prosperous, conservatively-dressed, middle-class blacks. However, Ike's following in California is mostly white, according to a Los Angeles Herald Examiner article. Quoting Kenneth Kolman, director of operations for the association: "Reverend Ike does not get involved with social activists such as civil rights issues. Reverend Ike lets his people know that he is not concerned with 'black power'; he is militant about only one thing; that is 'green power'." Reverend Ike stresses green power and faith healing in his sermons.[2] "I used to be black myself," says Ike, "Then I turned green." Ike is convinced that no one has to be poor, saying that the best thing one can do for the poor is not to be one of them. And when asked by

31

black militants what he's doing for black people, Ike's answer is given with equanimity: "The same thing I'm doing for white people. The greatest fallacy is that white folks need one thing and black folks something else. In this economy, it's money."

Reverend Ike is the first non-denominational radio preacher who is heard nationwide that has been classified with such flamboyant black preachers as Sweet Daddy Grace and Father Divine. In one sense, these observations are partly true, however, Reverend Ike is already better known than any of his famous predecessors and it seems that he could easily become the most famous and controversial black preacher in the history of American religion, with the possible exception of Martin Luther King, Jr.

He teaches his followers not to complain about the way that prices keep increasing. He says that instead they should say, "I give thanks for money to pay whatever price for whatever I need." Reverend Ike states that an individual should be quite careful in the way he talks and thinks about money. He admonishes them about saying that money is hard to get because if they say it is, money will be hard for them to obtain.[3]

When Reverend Ike first started preaching over the air about the gospel of wealth, his audience was primarily one which had been in the habit of listening to fundamental preaching; his message was somewhat strange to the people listening. However, they accepted him almost immediately because his program was short, only fifteen minutes, and they interpreted what he said as promoting the protestant work ethic. In other words, work hard and succeed; don't work and one does not get any food to eat.

As he became more accepted, Reverend Ike traveled all over the United States to hold healing and blessing meetings in auditoriums and coliseums. He sends postcards to those who have written for his literature and mailed announcements to those who have been using his "Blessing Plan," and advertises his scheduled meetings in their city. On the postcard, he notes that a special section will be set aside for those who are sick and disabled and those who have to come conveyed on stretchers, crutches or in wheelchairs, Reverend Ike conveyed the fact that he will walk down the aisle one hour before the meeting to meet and greet people personally — as many as possible. "I cannot talk after the meeting," he says. "I will need to catch my breath. Do not let any job or commitment keep you in slavery so that you cannot attend this meeting and be blessed with health, happiness, success and prosperity."[4]

At a meeting in Miami Beach, he told his followers:

I can love the Lord alot better when I've got money in my pocket, bless money. Money is God in action. Now I'm about to pray the prayer of success and prosperity. And as I pray, I'm going to receive the evening's offering. I don't want everyone to give —only those who see themselves having greater prosperity.[5]

When Reverend Ike was ready to collect the evening offering, he explained his highly unorthodoxed procedures:

Now I want those who can give $100.00 right now to come up to the front of this altar, and those of you who can't give $100.00, take out $50.00 and bring it up. . .and if you haven't got that, then take out a ten or a five. . .no change please (prefers a 'soft collection') . . .Hold those bills high, I want everyone to see your faith.[6]

Miami News Religious Editor

Wilcox, Miami News religious editor, said that he saw Ike's assistants goad people who remained seated in their chairs. They passed plastic pails among the crowd for their offering. They would not say how much money that they had collected, saying, "That's none of your business." They stated, "Our books are open to the federal government, not to the general public."

Reverend Ike, as the new Horatio Alger of broadcast preachers, is continuously spreading his message of success, through hard work or good luck, by public appearances all over the United States. He paid $25,000 to use the San Francisco Cow Palace for one night. One of the religious writers of a large syndicated religious column perceived him as "a comparatively new voice on the broadcast scene," and observed that Reverend Ike's costumes were as colorful as those that Liberace wore. Wilcox observed, in an article entitled "Ministry of Love Made Easier by $$," that the costume Ike wore was a "black and red-spangled double-breasted dinner jacket, pink ruffled shirt, red pants and red, white and black patent leather shoes."

People say that his money-raising techniques would make the late Sister Aimee McPherson turn pale. Moreover, his "jet-powered healing technique" would make Oral Roberts appear dignified.[7]

Reverend Ike bought a former New York City theatre in 1966 and set up his international headquarters. It cost more than $1 million for him to restore, furnish and decorate the giant building which now occupies a whole city block. Today it is called the United Palace. It has over 5,000 seats in the main auditorium. It also houses the educational facilities of the Science of Living Institute and Seminary, and the general offices of the United Christian Evangelistic Association which is run by Reverend Ike.

Reverend Ike says that the Science of Living Institute is not based on church doctrine or theology. He says that it is the teaching which equips a person:

> . . .to live a positive, dynamic, healthy, successful, prosperous life through the consciousness of the Presence of God — Infinite Good, already within every man. The Science of Living teaches you how to become a dynamic person. You unlearn sickness and know health. You unlearn poverty and know prosperity. Sickness, age, fear, worry, tension; every human torment drops away and a new you begins to live 'more abundantly'.[8]

On his television specials and during his regular Sunday services, Reverend Ike explains and propagates his philosophy by examining the books which he sells in his bookstore; his Science of Living contains metaphysical concepts that correlate to Religious Science. Along with this is a mixture of Norman Vincent Peale and Dale Carnegie.[9] Nevertheless, it is the presentation of his own philosophy in a vivifying and scintillating manner that causes his broadcast to appeal to thousands of people all over the United States.

Ben Kinchlow

Another black personality who deserves mention in this section is Ben Kinchlow who is neither a minister nor a gospel singer. He is the co-host of the Christian Broadcast Network's internationally syndicated "700 Club," which is telecast on over 150 stations in the United States.

On the one hand, Ben is a man that has no better perception than the next man. On the other hand, he looks at people in a way which is quite different from the manner that most people view others and which, in turn, causes people to see him in a different light. It is through the medium of Christian television that more and more people are looking at him.

He is quite a happy man and smiles for the thousands of people on the television throughout the North, South and Central America, and in many countries abroad. He was not this "happy" until he had a spiritual experience which caused the storms of his early life to subside. It resulted in the restoration of Ben's estranged wife and his family, and drew him from his job as a social worker with disadvantaged youth in Uvalde, Texas. He has become one of the newest black leaders in the tide of born-again Christianity that is causing revival in America today!

Ben's employment by CBN was like a "dream come true" for him. Yet not many years ago, his life was a nightmare of confusion, bitterness, hatred and crumbling relationship. When one sees him praying for CBN viewers or touching the audience with his unending humor and encompassing love, it is difficult to believe that this same man was once a follower of the Black Muslim activist, Malcolm X, who hated white people with a consuming passion. Today, however, he desires to help people of all ethnic and cultural backgrounds to find the revolutionary force that caused a spiritual change in his own life. Ben said that it was God's "incredible love and forgiveness through Jesus Christ," and that "only God that changed Ben Kinchlow."[10]

He was segregated in movie theatres and schools during the early part of his life. He said that he became aware that he was black when he attended an all-black school in San Antonio, Texas, which was taught by white nuns. His parents thought it was necessary for him to attend this school to obtain a good education. His differences from white students became even more apparent when, upon graduation, he received no scholarship offers from colleges although, at 6'4", he was quite an athlete. It was more important in those days to be white than talented and colleges were not too interested in getting black athletes for their teams.

Kinchlow's early experiences were quite important. They were the groundwork for what lay ahead for him. "One day a lady called me and asked if I would like to come to Dallas for the taping of "The 700" Club to tell what God was doing for us at Christian's Farms and for me personally. At that time, the program was being taped at different locations around the country. I said, "Sure, I'll go anywhere at any time to tell people about the love and forgiveness of Jesus Christ — so off I went," says Ben.

He went on the show, he was a hit with everyone and has remained until the present time. He is now director of special mail ministries. He spends weekends speaking to numerous groups all over the United States. He is working hard to introduce black Americans and all people everywhere to a new fulfilling way of life in Jesus Christ.[11]

Reverend Cleophus Robinson

Reverend Cleophus Robinson has made outstanding contributions to black religious broadcasting. According to Robinson, he is the oldest living gospel singer (Mahalia Jackson, Rosetta Thorpe and Joe Mays are deceased.) Robinson started his ministry more than 30 years ago with a live broadcast on KATZ in St Louis for Greater Bethlehem Baptist Church. He convinced station management that blacks in St. Louis should have a religious broadcast which would be sponsored by his church.

Robinson's telecasts have aired in approximately 75 cities on a periodic basis for the past 11 years. The programs have aired continuously in Seattle from 1968 to 1977. Seattle's KPLR requested him to start broadcasting there. In May of 1978 the program began airing in Puerto Rico and Hawaii which made Robinson the only black minister in telecasting outside the continental United States.[12]

"At this point," says Robinson, "I don't even know how many cities and towns the show is aired in because our program is on a number of cable stations." When asked why he felt other ministers had not tried to get on television, or those already on television had syndicated their programs, he said, "I guess that don't see the importance of reaching people who can't or won't go to church."

He has been featured on his gospel television show for 15 years on Channel 11 in St Louis — Sunday evenings and monday mornings. The weekly program is syndicated in 20 cities throughout the United States by his associates.[13]

Reverend Clay Evans

Reverend Clay Evans of Chicago is a great believer in electronic evangelism. He shares a one hour long telecast, "What A Fellowship" each Sunday on Chicago's Channel 38 and on about 23 other stations from Illinois to Atlanta and Tulsa to East Tennessee. Like both Robinson and Price, his video tapes are played on one station and then sent to another station.

Evans explains, "We prayed for this television ministry and God has blessed us." "What A Fellowship" is a program of fiery gospel music and spirit-filled preaching and what Evans refers to as the '3 P's' — praying, preaching and praising the Lord!"[14]

His telecast began two years ago as a half hour studio taped segment and, as community interest grew, so did the program. Its current hour-long format is of the worship service on Sunday mornings and airs from the Fellowship Missionary Baptist Church.

Evan's brand of ministry has attracted many youths. Now over 1,000 (one-fifth of his congregation) are young people 20 years of age and younger. Their participation helps the program communicate with the "now" generation.[15] When asked why he felt other churches have not been interested in being on television, Evans said, "It's costly, a very expensive endeavor." He also has been broadcasting on Chicago's WVON-AM for 26 years and his program airs on WXFN in Chicago and KWAM in Memphis.

Reverend Fred K. C. Price

Reverend Fred K. C. Price, pastor of Crenshaw Christian Center in Inglewood, California near Los Angeles, has a very unique television ministry; it's unlike any other religious telecast, black or white. The program, "Ever Increasing Faith," is an hour long sermon telecast from his church. There is not any singing or prayers, and no collection, nor even a request for money while the program is airing.

"I use the airways to share a unique spiritual experience with the viewer," says Price. "I believe people want to hear God's message, not see a church service. Mine is a teaching ministry. Our viewers and our stations like our approach to telecasting so much that we will be expanding our ministry to Boston and Jacksonville, Florida in 1979."

Price adds, "Our television programs are 58½ minutes and I teach for 56 of those minutes. We pay for all the telecasts ourselves and we don't have to depend on outside donations."[16]

He began broadcasting in 1970 primarily because of a spiritual experience. He had a vision to use radio and television to share the knowledge of the Bible with the public. "That experience changed my life and my ministry," he recalls. "I began to see that the Bible was real, it was alive and it would work for us today. It was not just a compilation of religious writings and traditional writings that we revere in reverence and it wasn't very far removed from our present time."

He continues, "I found that Jesus was very real. He is a very 'now' Jesus and unfortunately, he had never been presented that way in the traditional churches. I found that Jesus is now and God had given me a teaching ministry; although that ministry had not come before, because of spiritual lack, which was actually the lack of the holy spirit. When that happened, it was almost as though scales fell off my eyes. And so I began to teach and preach what God had shown me."

At the time of Price's vision, he had a small church of 100 members. Now his Crenshaw Christian Center has over 4500 persons on its membership rolls. It is the only black church in the Los Angeles area with four, full-time ministers, all making comfortable, livable salaries, according to Price.

He challenges his congregation, whose main attire is the Bible. Everyone brings his or her Bible each Sunday, and throughout the services, is continually searching from one scripture to the other. Some members take notes while others make notations in the margins of the Bibles and underscore verses. — "I challenge them (the congregation) to look things up in the Bible. Don't believe what I say or what anyone else says. I tell them to look it up for themselves. Then they can see that what I am saying is in fact what the Bible says, not just my opinion." says Price.

His telecast began airing on Trinity Broadcast Network, Channel 40 in April, 1978, on Friday and Sunday night. Less than one month later, he began telecasting on Metromedia Television Channel 11, one of Los Angeles' independent stations, on Sunday mornings. When asked why he chose to be on Channel 11 when he already was telecasting two hours on Channel 40, he explained that he wants his ministry to reach and be available to those persons who do not watch Christian and cable television stations.

In addition to Southern California, "Ever Increasing Faith" is seen in Arizona, Colorado, New Mexico, Texas, Georgia and Virginia. He also has a daily 15 minute program on two Los Angeles religious radio stations, KTYM and KFSG.

There is one interesting note about the ministries of Reverend Ike and Reverend Price. Both founded non-denominational churches. Could it be advantageous to increase black production of television programs by not being tied to the traditional dogma surrounding the various Christian denominations to which blacks belong? Both Robinson and Evans have used their involvement in gospel music and singing talents to broaden interest in their telecasts.

The First Black-Owned, Black-Operated Television Station in the United States of America

Undoubtedly, television plays a significant role in the lives of many Americans, and interestingly enough, the nation's only black television station, WGPR-TV, Channel 62, has a format which is 75 percent religious. Reverend Robert Grant, a member of the station's operations committee explains, "As a small, new station, we chose to go to that segment of the black community that could afford to telecast, and that was the churches."

The station began airing in September, 1978, and is owned and operated by WGPR, Inc., and headed by Dr. William Bands, who also serves as the station's general manager. According to Enicia Gregory, station manager, the religious programs on the station are mostly preaching and church services of Detroit ministers and churches. However, national syndicated programs, "PTL Club" and "Praise the Lord," air daily. There is also a Sunday gospel music show. WGPR, Inc. also owns WGPR-FM, the first black owned radio station in Michigan.

West

Reverend Clayton Russell was the black pioneer in religious broadcasting in Los Angeles. He was the first minister to begin broadcasting in 1936 on KFOX and was also the first black in Los Angeles to be on radio with his own show. Russell held this unique position for a number of years. His half hour morning church service has been on radio for 44 years. He had a 15 minute program and in the early 1940s, he was given public service time to broadcast on special days, such as Christmas, New Years and Easter, for many years.

Russell says that during World War II he used the airways to mobilize the community to become involved in the war effort. "After the war, I used the air time for civic and religious purposes, to talk about employment, housing and schools, because my ministry has always been concerned with the whole person, the spiritual and the material aspect of life," he added.

From 1942 to 1945, many of his programs were broadcast from a black owned cooperative supermarket in South Central Los Angeles. During the mid 1950s, he broadcast a 15-minute 'drive time' program at 8 a.m. consisting of sermonettes and singing with an organ accompaniment. He currently broadcasts a one hour church service called "Inspirational Hour" on KJLH on Sunday mornings.

KJLH is the second black-owned station west of the Mississippi River and was owned by John Hill and was sold to pop singer Steve Wonder in 1979. It broadcasts 14½ hours of religious programs on Sundays.

In 1970, Hill began with only six churches which increased little by little over the years. The churches do not pay a fee for broadcasting. The programs are sponsored by Hill's funeral home. He says, "I began having church services aired because my mother wanted to know what was going on at church but couldn't attend. I tried to give a cross-section of many denominations."

Nationally prominent, past president of the National Baptist Convention, the Reverend Dr. Thomas Kilgore, Jr. has been with the station since its first years. KJLH's "Church Direction 79," a half-hour talk show on Sundays, produced and hosted by Sam Coleman, is rapidly becoming a community favorite.

Two other secular stations have added a little spice to the gospel radio needs of the Los Angeles black community. Willie Davis' KACE broadcast three hours of inspirational message music and gospel music from 9 p.m. to midnight on Sundays. William E. Shearer, KACE general manger, says that this format was chosen to be competitive in the marketplace as well as to offer something to the community other than preaching and church services on Sunday evening.

Reverend Joseph Griffin is host of "The Church Today," a half-hour talk show on KGFJ, which began eight years ago. "This program is providing Southern Californians with an outlet to obtain a broader perspective of the religious affairs of the community," says Reverend Eugene Thomas, editor of *A.C.C. Church News* and first producer of "The Church Today." KGFJ is owned by the Inner City Broadcasting Company, a black firm in New York.

South and Southwest

Dr. William Holmes Borders, Sr., pastor of Wheat Street Baptist Church in Atlanta, began preaching on WGST in 1943. He was the first black minister in the South to begin regular broadcasting. His address, "Seven Minutes At The Mike in the Deep South," was broadcast in Atlanta overseas by Armed Forces Radio. In 1945, he began broadcasting on WERD. He says that he moved to WERD, a black-oriented station, because he had more freedom to say what he wanted to, and this station had a direct input to products and services sold to the black community of Atlanta. He continued airing on this station until 1975.

Dr. Borders began telecasting in 1978 on Channel 46. Shortly after initiating the telecast, the station's management asked him to do the program on a weekly basis. As his television program became more successful, Borders discontinued the radio broadcast.

Dr. Martin Luther King's church, Ebenezer Baptist Church in Atlanta, was the first black church to have a television program in Atlanta. It began in 1969 when Dr. King's brother, the late Reverend A. D. King. contacted WAGA, Channel 5, and convinced the management that his church should be allowed to telecast. From 1969 until his retirement in 1975, Daddy King, Reverend Martin Luther King, Sr., aired a half-hour program, according to Mrs. Sarah Reed, Ebenezer's secretary. Dr. Joseph L. Roberts, Jr., the church's current pastor, now does the broadcast which is videotaped in the studio. This includes a sermonette and music from the various Ebenezer choirs. In 1979, Ebenezer received national attention via television, as it had done in the 1960's when Dr. King was living, when Coretta Scott King was presented with an award by President Jimmy Carter on her husband's birthday.

Another nationally prominent minister in Atlanta, Reverend Ralph David Abernathy of West Hunter Street Bapitist Church, for 15 years has broadcast a one-hour program on radio. He is currently on WYZE, Sunday afternoons.

One of Atlanta's religious stations, WXLL, is oriented to black audiences. It is providing new opportunities for black ministers to broadcast and allows the community to hear gospel music each day.

Irene Johnson Ware of Mobil, Alabama's WTOK has made several unique contributions as a black, religious broadcaster. In 1960, she began her broadcasting career at WTOK as a receptionist/announcer and is now the station's manager; the first black woman in the South to manage a radio station. She is also the gospel editor of *Black Radio Exclusive*. Ware has been one of the most active voices for the perpetuation and promotion of gospel music across the country. She has been national director (gospel division) of several record companies; vice president of Jewel Records, and isa part owner of Po-Rene Products, Ltd., a firm which promotes gospel concerts.

Reverend Charles Jackson of Pleasant Grove Church in Houston began telecasting in 1974. According to Blanch Ranger, church secretary, Pleasant Grove was the first church in Houston to have a continuous telecast.

From 1974 to August 1978, it telecasted a one-hour program on Channel 29 on Sundays. "Our program is now a half hour, 10 to 10:30 p.m. on Sundays," says Ranger. "It consists of a sermonette, prayers and music, and is taped in a studio. The program is also telecast in Louisiana and also Northern and Eastern Texas."

Pleasant Grove has been on radio since the early 1940s. Reverend

A. A. McCardell, the church's former pastor, began doing a half-hour show on KYOK, then moved to KCOH.

Several Texans have indicated that the first black minister in Texas to have a religious broadcast in the early 1940s was Bishop R. E. Ranger of Fort Worth.

East

Dr. B. Samuel Hart is the owner of WYIS in Phoenixville near Philadelphia and was the nation's first black evangelical to own a radio station. WYIS was the first black-owned station in the Delaware Valley of Pennsylvania. WYIS began airing in August, 1978 and is a daytime-only station.[17]

Hart is also president of the Grand Old Gospel Fellowship, Inc., which produces the "Grand Old Gospel Hour," heard on 130 radio stations in the United States and 5 foreign countries. The program has aired since 1962. In 1976, the "Grand Old Gospel Hour" received the Aware of Merit from the National Religion Broadcasters Association (NRB) for setting a standard of excellence in broadcasting to black audiences.

Becoming Phoenixville's first radio station and the first black-owned religious station was no easy task. It took several years for Hart's dream to become a reality. It took over two years from the time he filed his application with the FCC in June, 1976 to the day his first program was broadcast in August, 1978.

He had zoning, licensing and leasing difficulties. Each of the problems he overcame. "We just took each transaction a step at a time," says Hart. "Even after the FCC granted the license in 1977, which meant we could begin broadcasting, we still had to construct the radio towers and handle many other minute items."

Hart has never been one to dodge the challenge of a difficult task. A native of Harlem and the son of missionaries, he was brought up in Jamaica. He was active early in his career in the Boston area where he founded and established two youth organizations, a children's camp and a church. After moving to Philadelphia, he established eight churches and a summer camp for youth.

He was also the first black to be elected to the National Religious Broadcaster Association's Board of Directors.

The Reverend Benjamin Smith, Sr., the pastor of Deliverance Evangelistic Church, made his mark on religious telecasting in 1978 with a new

42

program, Time of Deliverance. According to Martha Addison, 'Time of Deliverance' producer, Smith began telecasting on WPHL, Channel 17, in Philadelphia in June. By October, he became the first black minister to use the Praise the Lord Network's (PTL) satellite system.

Prior to becoming affiliated with PTL, 'Time of Deliverance' was seen only in Chicago, Allentown and Philadelphia, Pennsylvania. "Now," says Addison, "the program is viewed in 94 cities in 30 states." She adds, "Our non-denominational church has a broad outreach ministry, of which the telecast is only one portion. Reverend Smith understands that television and radio are excellent vehicles to reach people and share the gospel. "Television is a very popular medium with black people." Smith also broadcasts daily, 15-minute radio programs which air in Camden, New Jersey, Odessa, Texas, and Denver, Colorado.

Dr. Ernie Wilson of Church Centered Evangelism in Philadelphia has done numerous programs during his many years as a broadcaster. During many of his 20 trips to Africa, Wilson has shared his unique broadcast with the people of that land. His evangelistic efforts and broadcasts have also spread to Latin America, Bermuda and the Bahamas. He is a member of the NRB Board of Directors.

Midwest

James Massy is speaker on the Christian Brotherhood Hour Church of God (Anderson, Indiana). Appointed for a five-year term in 1977, he is the first black to hold the position as speaker during the many years the program has aired. This broadcast can be heard in more than 400 cities across the United States, and nine foreign countries.

On Detroit television, Ed Smith, former gospel disc jockey and executive secretary of the Gospel Music Workshop, was the first black to have a religious telecast in Detroit. From 1970 to 1976, he hosted the "Motor City Golden Gospel" on WJBK-TV. Smith says, "The show was quite popular. There was no preaching. It was like a variety show with gospel singing groups, music and poetry."[18]

Brother Ed's involvement in religious broadcasting also touched radio on WGPR-FM where he was religious coordinator and assisted with the airing of about 30 hours of Sunday and daily programs. He was also a gospel announcer of WJLB.

The Reverend C. L. Franklin, father of popular recording artist Aretha Franklin, is also a singer. And, according to Reverend Franklin's director of Christian education, he has been broadcasting for 28 years and was probably the first black minister on radio in Detroit. His evening worship service on WJLB has been a focal point in Detroit for many gospel recording artists and the community since the 1940s.

The late Reverend Clarence Cobb, pastor of First Church of Deliverance in Chicago, had the unique distinction of having the oldest, continuous broadcast on the same station in the entire midwest. For 32 years, his midnight church service on WCFL was the program to listen to, especially when one wanted to hear top gospel singers like Sally Martin and Mahalia Jackson, as well as today's contemporary gospel artists. His fiery broadcasts with lusty choirs singing are probably the most famous in gospel music. [19]

Since WCFL is a 50,000 watt station and is usually heard far from Chicago, interested listeners in Wisconsin, Michigan, Indiana and as far south as Cairo, Illinois and Kentucky could easily tune into the station. Consequently, Cobb built a loyal following in four or five states and has only had to pay for time on one station, namely WCFL.

The Reverend Garfield Hubbard is reported to be the first black on KATZ radio in the greater St. Louis area. His church is Morning Star in East St. Louis, Illinois and currently he is on WESL radio. Reverend Cleophus Robinson, however, was the first minister in the St. Louis area to be on television.

East

Dr. J. Morgan Hodges of Washington and Reverend Joseph Brown of Baltimore, directors of Ethnic Broadcasting Foundation, are the first broadcasters to have a radio station in a correctional institution at Lorton Reformatory. This is a non-commercial station and is used mostly as a training program for inmates. [20]

Both Brown and Hodges have been involved in broadcasting for many years. Brown's "Grace Memorial Hour" is currently airing in 120 countries around the world via shortwave radio. Hodges, one of the first black newsmen for CBS does not broadcast at this time. He serves as chairman of the NRB's Ethnic Broadcasters Committee.

For 40 years, the "Man with a Message," Bishop Smallwood Williams of Washington, D.C., has been continuously broadcasting on WINX. His message has gained numerous loyal listeners, so much so that he is heard on five other stations. He has also been on WNJR, Trenton, New Jersey, for 20 years and has aired internationally in Liberia for 10 years.

44

Television in Washington and Balimore is still an area where blacks doing religious broadcasting have not appeared on a regular basis.

The Communications Commission of the National Council of Churches sponsors two programs that air primarily over NBC affiliates. These programs are "National Radio Pulpit" and "Art of Living." Three black ministers have opened the door for the other blacks. They are: Dr. William A. Jones, Bethany Baptist Church, Brooklyn; Dr. Garnder C. Taylor, Concord Baptist Church, Brooklyn; and Dr. Henry Mitchell, Director of the Ecumenical Center for Black Church Studies in Los Angeles. Jones was on both programs in 1975 and 1977. Taylor was the first to be on Art of Living in 1959. He appeared again in 1970. Mitchell appeared on National Radio Pulpit in 1978.

The significance of their appearing is the longevity of their programs and their broad listening audiences. NBS's National Pulpit is the oldest religious program on the air. It has been airing for 56 years, since 1923.[21]

Dr. Jones' credits as a broadcaster are a little different than those of most black ministers. For three years, he was co-host of "Religion on the Line" on New York's WMAC, a two-hour, call-in talk show. Three clergymen of different faiths would share hosting responsibilities on the program. Jones would share a Protestant point of view with callers, while a rabbi and a Catholic priest would share their respective points of view each week of the broadcast. Jones has aired 12 sermons on Family Radio's "Conference Echos." His sermons are aired at no cost to him over 12 stations across the United States. According to some New Yorkers, Jones also has the largest radio listening audience for his one-hour broadcast than any church (black or white) in New York. It airs on Sunday evenings, WFME-FM radio. Because of the broad signal of the station, Jones' broadcast can be heard in New Jersey, Connecticut and Upstate New York.

On the gospel disc-jockey side of things in New York, Joe Bostick is a name that can be remembered as far back as 1939. Bostick is considered the "Dean of Gospel Music."[22] He aired a Sunday show and a daily one-half hour show called "Gospel Train" on WCNW for 10 years. This was long before most other disc jockeys were thinking about gospel music. In 1949, he moved to WLIB and continued to draw more loyal listeners. Bostick's fame and outreach were greater than his station's airwaves. People would come to hear his gospel concerts from as far away as Boston and Baltimore. He began promoting gospel concertsin the early 1940s, something that was unheard of at that time. Two of his most notable achievements were his bringing Mahalia Jackson to Carnegie Hall in 1951 and his making her one of the headliners at the Newport Jazz Festival in 1957.

One other New Yorker is Harlem minister and gospel singer Wyatt Walker. At the request of the German News Agency in New York, Walker's church services were taped and aired via radio in West Germany, Sweden and Italy.

Father Paul A. Gopaul was the first black Catholic priest to do a continuous radio program. From 1952 to 1956, he did a half-hour show, "Design for Christian Living" on WJOY in Vermont.

World Community of Al Islam in the West

The number of Christian programs aimed toward the black community is on the increase. The World Community of Al Islam in the West (formerly the Nation of Islam) has also increased the number of stations on which its programs have broadcast since the early 1960s.

According to Wallace Muhammad, broadcast consultant for the Community, the organization currently airs on 70 to 80 stations and have aired on more than 100 at various times. In the early years of the broadcast, the message was given by the Honorable Elijah Muhammad, founder of the Community, and then Malcolm X did the broadcast. During those years, Elijah Muhammad continued to broadcast on Chicago stations while Malcolm X was heard in other cities. From approximately 1965 to 1975, Minister Louis Farrakham was the spokesman. When Chief Imam Wallace Dean Muhammad assumed the top leadership position of the Community in 1975, he became the spokesman and did the broadcast.

The local station and timing for each broadcast is arranged by the believers in that locality to provide better rapport and continuity with local station management. "All the broadcasts are paid for and only about 10 percent are public service time," says Wally Muhammad . The program is formatted much like Christian shows. There is primarily a single speaker sharing his thoughts and ideas with the listener. The broadcast is currently aired internationally in Bermuda, Trinidad and Belize, Central America.[23]

In Chicago, Wally Muhammad broadcasts "The Communicator," a weekly show on WBEE. He describes this Moslem program as "contemporary inspirational music" with inspirational thoughts. It is a program of music with a message and talks about Moslem and Christian leaders, like Martin Luther King, Jr. It features the poetry of some prominent black poets and of little known poets as well.

46

International

In the international marketplace, blacks are making new strides. Dr. Howard O. Jones, associate evangelist with the Billy Graham Evangelistic Association, has been broadcasting internationally for more than 25 years on ELWA in Monrovia, Liberia. He began in 1954; soon he was receiving responses to the broadcast from all over West Africa.[24]

Not only has Jones been actively involved in his overseas broadcast, his wife, Wanda, has done special programs oriented to women. His daughters, the Jones Sisters, well known recording artists on Ultimate Records, also appeared on television programs geared toward youthful audiences in the Billy Graham crusades, Day of Discovery television programs, and they still participate in his broadcast ministry.[25]

Jones' "Hour of Freedom" is heard in the United States, South Africa, Eastern Europe, Russia, China and other countries. Jones was the winner of the 1980 National Religious Broadcasters Association's Award of Merit for excellence in broadcasting. He started "Hour of Freedom" 33 years ago in New York on Saturday nights with a program primarily for young people and now his voice is heard around the world. He is one of three blacks who serve on the NRB's Board of Directors and is the only black to serve on the NRB's Executive Committee.

Many other blacks are also broadcasting internationally. Ben Kinchlow of the Christian Broadcast Network's 700 Club is seen on 34 countries around the world. Dr. B. Samuel Hart's "Grand Old Gospel Hour" is broadcasted in Puerto Rico, West Africa, India and the Antilles. The Reverend Samuel Williams, president of the National Negro Evangelist Association of Oregon, airs "Redemption Hour" via Transworld Radio to several countries.

The World Community of Al Islam on the West broadcasts in Barbados, Belize, Bermuda and Trinidad. Washington's Bishop Smallwood Williams has been broadcasting over Liberia's EWLA for over 10 years.

Black, All Gospel Stations

WYIS, near Philadelphia, boarsts the largest coverage of any Christian AM commercial station in the country. With 160 miles of clear coverage, it has the capability of reaching millions in eastern and central Pennsylvania, New Jersey and Delaware.

"Conservative Christian programming and top quality programming for blacks are the basic features of WYIS," says Hart, owner of WYIS. "We call ourselves 'Wise Radio,' for he that winneth souls is wise."[26]

Washington, D.C.'s WYCB began broadcasting about the same time as WYIS in August, 1979. However, WYCB is different from every other station in the United States because of its format of black-oriented, contemporary, inspirational/religious music.[27]

The station's general manager, Howard Sanders, explains: "We're not promoting Christianity, we're trying to promote spirituality and inspire blacks to do things to change their lives to a positive direction." "WYCB also treats news differently by placing emphasis on positive local news, not on national and international items," says J. T. Smith, WYCB's former program director.

The station also broadcasts several unique public affairs items: an interview program hosted by the Council of Churches of Greater Washington, a "Martin Luther King, Jr. Tribute," which includes 10 to 30-second shorts about his life, two-minute excerpts of King's speeches which are aired at various times during the broadcast day, and 30 to 60 minute speeches of King at noon and at 8 p.m.

WYCB was the 55th black-owned station in the country and the first in Washington, D.C. It is owned by Washington Community Broadcasting.

KTYM in Inglewood, near Los Angeles, is formatted for a black audience during the week and has a foreign language format on weekends. Gerado Borrego, general manager, says that the station began this dual format in 1958 because of its location (ghetto of Inglewood/Los Angeles) and because its management chose to be non-competitive with other white-oriented religious stations and black rhythm and blues stations. KTYM stays afloat with its unusual format.

Robert Hardway, program director, laughingly shares that KTYM is the only station in the country which airs religious programs in English, Japanese, Russian, Rumanian, German and Italian that has a black program director.

KTYM gospel disc-jockey Reverend Ray Branch agrees with Hardway that much of KTYM's success is due to its unique format and the increased taste for black gospel music.

A former gospel songwriter and musician, Hardway explains that of the 16 black ministers on the station each week, seven have a daily 15 minute program. They are: Reverends Reben Anderson, E. E. Cleveland, Eddie Jerigan, M. L. Rayford, O. O. Wolfe, Pastor Catherine McFarland and Reverend Fred Price, who also has two television programs. Some KTYM listeners say that the variety and the kind of preaching that these ministers do has also contributed to KTYM's increased black audience.

The Honorable Elijah Muhammad, World Community of Islam in the West (formerly The Nation of Islam) has broadcast a half hour program on KTYM for four years.

WUST, a daytime station, chose a black gospel format in 1970 due to a very competitive Washington, D.C. radio market. It has a daily format of approximately 30 percent talk which includes church services, preaching and a call-in interview talk show. Cal Hackett, program director, explains: "WUST was the first station in Washington to make the airway available to the black community via the call-in talk show which airs (afternoons) Monday through Friday." Gospel music is broadcasted for the remainder of the day. There are four black ministers who have daily programs. The station also does Mutual Black Network News.

The state of Georgia has two all religious stations that compete for the attention of the black listeners. They are WEAS in Savannah and WXLL in Atlanta. WEAS's format is oriented toward the white and black communities. One-third of the day, late afternoon, is black gospel music and black preachers are featured while white gospel music and white ministers are featured during the rest of the day.

WXLL, also a sunrise to sunset station, went to an all gospel format in 1978. Its broadcast day consists of 30 to 40 percent talk, including preaching and the remainder is music. There are mostly church services on Sunday, aired live from the church sanctuaries. Four local black ministers air 15 minute daily programs. WXLL also has hourly news from the ABC Information Network.

KMAX in Pasadena is geared to a black audience. Darby Cunningham, KMAX's general manager, says that his station plays more black gospel music than any other station in the Los Angeles market. Ollie Collins, Los Angeles' top gospel disc jockey, has a very unique morning drive time gospel music show. In addition to playing the most popular hits and old favorites, listeners can call in and voice their opinions on the air on subjects related to the day's topic; such as dating, life after death, divorce, etc. Collins, a former gospel singer, explains that his early morning show is successful because he gives his listeners what they want to hear and provides them with inspirational music and conversation which helps them make it through the day.

The station airs gospel music and foreign language public affairs in the afternoon. There are three black ministers that air daily programs.

"KMAX tries to provide black churches with an opportunity to broadcast and we have many storefront churches and a few medium-sized churches broadcasting their services," says Cunningham. "The television program, 'Roots,' made people want to hang onto their culture. KMAX tries to provide its listeners with that kind of opportunity. We believe that we provide this 'Roots' feeling through airing our program to Black, Chinese, Vietnamese, Laotian, Cambodian, Dutch and Indian audiences."

CHAPTER VI

SATELLITE SPACE RACE

The space race is on. Religious broadcasters are using those big transmitters in the sky to tell the world about the Lord. These transmitters, called satellites, orbit the earth, making it possible to reach millions of people 24 hours a day.

Challenging The "Big Three"

The Christian Broadcasting Network (CBN), the largest religious programming source in religious broadcasting today, uses the RCA Satcom II Satellite. In addition, the network has numerous satellite earth stations for broadcasting to the 60 largest United States markets. These disc receivers have allowed CBN to telecast to every section of the United States.

Located in Virginia Beach, Virginia, CBN has become an ever expanding, worldwide broadcasting network and is making efforts to establish a fourth network as an alternative to the "Big Three" (ABC, NBC, CBS). Pat Robertson, Chief Executive of this electronic evangelical empire, says that the major networks are dominated by sex, violence and secular humanism. He is determined to offer something different. He will fulfill what he believes to be his God-given mission. He states, "TV does not mirror society's problems. It has become the problem. The lifestyles it shows are destructive of society and so we plan to project a climate of decency and wholesomeness. We think there is a ready-made audience for it."

Robertson is the son of Senator A. Willis Robertson of Virginia, a Golden Gloves boxer, Marine combat officer in Korea, Phi Beta Kappa, Yale Law School graduate, and an ordained minister who once performed his ministry in Brooklyn.[1] He began broadcasting over WYAH, a UHF station in Portsmouth, Virginia. The call letters of the station stand for the name, Yahweh (making it the first television station to be called by the

Hebrew name of God). It is the flagship station of CBN's broadcasting system which has independent stations WANX in Atlanta, WXNE in Boston and, its most profitable station, KXTX in Dallas. The CBN owns six radio stations; one in Norfolk and five others in New York State.[2]

Robertson founded CBN on January 11, 1960 (the date its charter was filed) and he opened a bank account with a deposit of three dollars, promptly overdrawing it by ordering a six dollar checkbook. In November of 1960, the FCC granted CBN a permit for the first television station in America scheduled to broadcast 50 percent or more in religious time. (The late evangelical Percy Crawford bought a Philadelphia station in the fifties, but it went under financially, failing to achieve the quality of religious programming he envisioned.)[3]

Today, twenty years later, CBN's programs are in all 50 states and in 25 foreign countries, over approximately 200 television stations and 165 radio stations. It is also carried into 4,000 communities via cable television. The CBN's success has made it possible for Robertson to obtain affiliation agreements with approximately 90 television and 120 radio stations that wish to be a part of the fourth network.

The major networks, however, appear not to be too worried by the plans of CBN becoming a viable network. An ABC official, who said that he wished the religious broadcasters well, says that they were "only a dot" on the commercial network's horizon. Not only do they not have anywhere near the billions of dollars the commercial networks command but also they are networks in name only. That is, they do not have relationships similar to that which each of the commercial networks enjoy with their 200 or so affiliated stations. Instead, the religious networks must rely on cable and independent stations that can pick and choose at will among the programs offered free by CBN and others.[4]

Robertson explains that CBN is well on its way to becoming fully competitive with the "Big Three," but won't be taken seriously until it reaches $1 billion of annual income. Once CBN gets all of its earth stations operating, the network affiliates will be fair game because many of them are dissatisfied with the policies of the large networks and CBN will welcome an alternative.

CBN can currently supply affiliates a package of religious programs produced by the network that amount to as much as forty hours a week of programming. These programs vary from situation comedies to sports, news to Christian soap operas, and "The 700 Club," CBN's flagship program, a variety show.

"The 700 Club" began in 1963 when Robertson decided to hold a telethon to raise money to keep his then fledgling network afloat. He had calculated that he needed $7,000 a month to meet expenses, so he appealed for 700 people who would pledge ten dollars each month. In a moment of inspiration, he called the telethon "The 700 Club."[5]

In addition to heading up CBN as its president, Robertson is host of "The 700 Club." His style and the format of the show are far afield of what other religious broadcasters like Billy Graham or Oral Roberts have. He tends to remind one more of Merv Griffin or Johnny Carson. His television setting even resembles the "Tonight Show." He has a painted cityscape in the background which is framed by gothic-arched windows.[6]

Pat sits behind a typical talk show desk with his enthusiasm-builder and co-host, Ben Kinchlow, a former Black Muslim, seated to his right.[7] They don't preach, but allow their guests to share their personal religious experiences and the role of God in their lives. "We simply took a format that had worked on the commercial networks and applied it to CBN," Robertson says. "It was a proven format that had reached millions of Americans."

In another part of the CBN studio, a battery of "prayer counselors" are answering telephone calls from viewers sharing their problems and concerns with the counselors. "The 700 Club" pioneered this concept of "two-way television" that is just beginning to catch on in regular commercial television.

The satellite system is the key to CBN's growing success. In April of 1977, CBN signed a six million dollar, six year agreement with RCA American Satellite Corporation to relay its religious programs to the cable system, which offers CBN programs free of charge.

Robertson says that some CBN programs are beamed off the RCA SATCOM II Satellite to a receiving disc in the nation's top sixty markets. CBN transmits twenty-four hours a day, reaching six million cable homes. The network has established itself as the largest syndicator of satellite transmitted programs in the United States.

In 1979, "The 700 Club" was telecast in the Holy Land via Israel Cable Television Limited, making it the first religious program to be aired in Israel in English. That same year, CBN joined forces with George Otis Ministries to build a radio station in Southern Lebanon and will be heard in many Middle Eastern countries.[8]

Robertson took on one more responsibility in 1978 as founding president of CBN University, a new graduate college offering Master's degrees in communications and theology, with programs in music, drama, business, government and law to be added at a later time. Thousands of perspective students applied for admission to the school which initially began with around two hundred students. However, CBN's expansion to its new twenty million dollar Virginia Beach site has provided much more space to accommodate scores of additional students.

CBN can also be credited for telecasting the nation's first all religious television news program, "New Sight." This program began in November of 1979 and is produced by students of CBN University's graduate school of communication. The thirty minutes of news is aired twice weekly. It includes hard news, special reports, features and editorial comments.[9]

William Martin states, in an article entitled "Heavenly Host" in *Texas Monthly Magazine*, that:

> Some people who question the salutory effects of religion, especially in its theologically conservative and behaviorally enthusiastic forms, find it difficult to believe that men like Robertson and Roger Baerwolf (General Manager of KXTX in Dallas), who talk so easily about God, are not, at worst, slipping considerable sums (of money) into their well-tailored pockets or at least wasting money that could be better spent.[10]

Robertson countered this outlook by saying, "that if someone goes to live in the jungle or lives alone in the woods, he is okay but if someone wears a business suit and has a staff and does what is needed to reach people in today's civilized world, they are immediately awed by the numbers involved. They have a stereotyped image of what they think a holy man should be like and if he doesn't fit that image, something must be wrong. They can see taking a hundred million dollars and feeding some hungry people, but they can't see using that money for the communication of thought. People have to understand that intangibles are of value. Truth is a thing of value, peace and long-suffering and mercy and gentleness — these are of great value to the nation, and the only way they can be transmitted is through the spoken word and to do that in a high-speed, fast-moving, industrialized society requires large sums of money relative to the cost of running the little brown church in the wildwood."[11]

To keep from misleading you, Martin did end his article by stating that he felt comfortable with Robertson and CBN. He said, "I came away from Dallas and Virginia Beach convinced that I had been talking to people who not only have hung a new star in the heavens but who also believe in what they say and practice what they preach."

CBN's quest to become the fourth network becomes a greater reality each day. I think one would be hard pressed to disagree with many of the items that CBN lists in its April 1978 issue of *The Flame*. The reasons they list as the need for the fourth network were:

Here's Why America Needs a Fourth Network

According to Mass Media Ministries, the average American TV set is used more than six hours a day.

By the time children are graduated from high school, they have spent 50 percent more time watching TV than in school.

Children watch television on the average of 20-25 hours a week.

According to United Methodist Communications, 98 percent of all American homes have working television sets.

According to *Television/Radio Age International*, there are 135 million television sets in this country, or about three sets for every five persons.

There are an estimated 50 million television sets in the Soviet Union, 26 million in Japan, 19 million in West Germany, 14 million in France, 18 million in Great Britain, 13 million in Italy, 10 million in Canada, and 9 million in Brazil.

There were no television sets in the Far East in 1945. By 1955, there were seven stations in that part of the world; by 1964, 841.

Producing a 30-second product commercial for television typically costs $60,000-$70,000 and can run significantly more.

The Surgeon General's Office reports that more than 80 percent of all prime time programs contain aggression, with an average of seven overt acts of aggression per hour on the major networks.

A year-end report by the U. S. Conference of Mayors reports that weapons ranging from clubs to handguns appear an average of nine times every hour on prime-time TV. Such weapons appeared 648 times in a 73-hour sample.

Television advertising grew from a $300 million business in 1952 to $6 billion in 1976. In one three month period alone, almost 100 advertisers spent more than $1 million each on TV spot commercials. This is from a research study done by the State University of New York.

An FCC spokesman estimates that half a billion dollars is spent annually on advertising in children's TV alone.

Most children begin to watch television at age 2½. By age 7, 94 percent view regularly. According to one survey, fewer than 50 percent of all mothers of first graders ever make occasional television selections for thier children. Thirty percent never supervise their children's viewing choices. An estimated 5 million children under 12 still are watching television by midnight, according to a study by the National PTA.

It has been estimated that between the ages of 5 and 15, the average child will watch the televised destruction of more than 13,400 people.

A 1974 poll by *U.S. News and World Report* of 1,000 national leaders revealed that television, in the opinion of those polled, was the single most powerful institution in America.

The 3,895 AM and 1,136 FM radio stations in America broadcast an average of 730,000 commercials a day; 770 television stations broadcast 100,000 commercials a day.

The *Christian Science Monitor* examined 240 programs and found that 80 percent involved the use of alcohol either in ads or the scripts.

In the past year, the number of complaints citizens have filed with the FCC on obscenity, indecency and profanity have risen from 6,143 to 20,146.

Challenging CBN

Making a very competitive effort to outdistance the Christian Broadcasting Network to become the fourth network, and with the potential of becoming the largest Christian television network in the country, according to some informed sources — is the Tustin, California based, Trinity Broadcasting Network (TBN).

Reverend Paul Crouch, Founder and General Manager of the burgeoning network, says that TBN broadcasts its first program from a dimly lit studio using a single borrowed camera and some makeshift scenery in May 18, 1973 and has grown to be the world's largest producer and distributor of Christian programming. This they became in only five short years.

On May 15, 1977, TBN became the first full, twenty-four hour, one hundred percent Christian television station in the world. It operates from two sound stages and a mobile studio at its Tustin facility. The station is on the air seven days a week and almost around-the-clock. It generally closes only for three and a half hours on Sundays. Some 67 regular series are originated from the facilities, both videotaped and live, according to Carl McMillian, TBN Director of Engineering.[12]

TBN uses some syndicated programming, however there is substantial commitment to new origination. The non-denominational broadcasting network operates without grants or the specific support of any church or religious association.

Since the public continuously questions funds taken in by religious broadcasters, TBN management say that they welcome any questions about the network's revenues and Crouch freely offers to disclose the network's income as he points to the Romans 12:17 scripture: "Provide things honest in the sight of all men." Crouch adds, "All religious organizations should make full and free disclosures. We've been doing it for four years. Before that there wasn't really much to disclose."[13]

A native of Missouri, Crouch began in broadcasting in 1956 as a country-western disc jockey at a Rapid City, South Dakota radio station and he also served as Associate Pastor of a local Assembly of God church.

Crouch helped to pioneer and build Channel 7, an NBC affiliate in Rapid City and moved up to become its program director after being there only three months. He explains that he got the job as program director, not because he was qualified to be but because everyone else had resigned and moved onto "greener pastures."

He moved to Southern California, becoming General Manager of radio station KREL in Corona, buying part interest in the station. In 1970, he sold his Corona interest, taking up the same duties at KHOF in Glendale, California. He left after two years to organize TBN.[14]

Cheaper Transmitters

In 1978, TBN received permission from the Federal Communications Commission for earth-to-satellite transmission and receiving stations in California and Arizona. According to Tim Flynn, KTBN Program Director, the revolutionary aspect of this hinges on the FCC's recent authorization to "feed translator stations" which pick up television signals from space satellites and then retransmit them on a different channel locally. Since the transmitters cost only thirty thousand dollars each, TBN can locate television transmission sites in scores of cities relatively inexpensively.

The catch, Flynn points out, is that the FCC requires that signals broadcast by translator stations must be the re-transmission of live broadcasts by stations everywhere. Pre-packaged programs, therefore, could not be rerun by this method. TBN set out right away, as did other Christian networks, using this new authorization to its advantage. On May 1, 1978, TBN telecast, live and direct, from the Mount of Olives in Jerusalem, Israel, where many evangelical Christians think Jesus will appear in his Second Coming. The program included interviews with Moshe Dayan, hero General of the Israeli nation, and Jerusalem Mayor Teddy Kollek.[15]

Crouch hosted the "Praise the Lord" show, the signature program of TBN, which airs across the United States and in Puerto Rico, Guatemala and Haiti. It has the same Johnny Carson format as CBN's "The 700 Club." TBN's viewers can also call and request a prayer, make monetary pledges or just have someone to talk to. This program and many of TBN's other productions, for adults and children, are on the TBN network, plus a wide variety of programs produced by leading ministries across the United States.[16]

TBN's expansive marketing campaigns have already reached over 6,000 cable stations offering programs to them free of charge. The "Let's Praise the Lord" program is viewed on over 1,500 cable stations that have their own receive-only satellite earth stations. Hundreds more have already applied to the FCC and are planning to install the needed facilities as soon as they receive permission.

TBN's insistence on high quality, Christian programming, has caused many stations to request permission to carry TBN programs. These "so-called" affiliate stations will be able to receive these programs via satellite much cheaper than they could if they were required to ship their programs by videotape. In fact, it would be virtually impossible to ship all of the programs to these markets.

The word "translator" has worked its way into the vocabulary of many Americans and many Christians. The FCC passed a rule in 1978 allowing translators which are small (100 and 1,000 watt repeater broadcast stations) to be fed via satellite. The result of this ruling is that a broadcast station can economically broadcast into remote areas that were normally inaccessible to its broadcast facility. For example, if there is a mountain range between a city and TBN's transmitter which prevents the city from receiving the station's signal, the people in that geographical zone can join together and raise the money to install a translator on a mountain overlooking the city. Since the translator is located high in the mountain, the translator can receive TBN's signal and then repoint and retransmit it down to the city.[17]

In most cases translators have only been located near the broadcast station. Now the FCC allows stations to feed their signal to the satellite to a low-cost-low-power, easy-to-license translator.

This means that a city on the east coast, like Wilmington, Delaware, can have its own translator and receiver-only earth stations and thereby receive the signal of TBN. Instead of the cost of one million dollars to build a full, high-powered broadcast station in the city, the cost of the translator is under $40,000. Formerly, only large cities in the United States could afford a full-time Christian station. Now even the smallest communities can have it.[18]

Trinity Broadcasting Network has made tremendous strides since going on the air in 1973. Most of its revenues come from donations and the rest from production and time sales. It continues to be a front-runner in the satellite space race and the competitors vying to become the fourth network.

Challenging Everybody

The Praise The Lord (PTL) network, based in Charlotte, North Carolina, is also in the satellite space race. Headed by Jim Bakker, a former partner with TBN's head, Paul Crouch, the PTL (also known as People That Love) emphasizes inspirational and evangelistic programming and a talk show format. Bakker started the two hour talk program in 1974. It looks more like Carson's Tonight Show than any of its religious broadcasting competitors.

Bakker wears flashy suits and jokes with his Ed McMahon-like co-host, Harry Harrison.[19] Several times a week he may go off stage into a rap with the studio audience. The viewers love it and beg for more. Bakker started the PTL Club with sixty dollars in his pocket. Now the show is carried by more than 213 affiliates and aired on over 3,000 cable systems. According to *Variety Magazine*, the PTL Club is the most viewed daily television program in the world. In the short span of seven years, PTL has grown from a local program to an international network. In 1979 alone, PTL purchased nearly fifteen and a half million dollars worth of air time.

An all-Spanish show, "Club PTL," produced at the Heritage Village Studios (the PTL Headquarters), is sent by video cassette into eighteen Spanish speaking countries. It has top ratings in four countries. Similar to the PTL Club format, the Spanish version, hosted by Juan Romero, has testimonies in the style for which PTL is known. With offices in Panama, Club PTL also features well-known artists and is having a significant effect on both the Roman Catholic and Protestant churches in these developing nations.

Nigerian evangelist, Reverend Benson Idahosa, is the host of the

59

African "PTL Club", which is viewed in Ghana, Liberia and, weekly, in Nigeria. PTL's Entr'Amis (Among Friends) with Roland Cosnard hosting, is telecast in France, Belgium and Luxemburg. Sam Arai hosts pilot programs of the Japanese version of PTL. "I don't believe in tokenism. The gospel must be communicated to people in their language, consistent with their own culture," says Bakker. There are also programs in Thailand and Australia which are hosted by nationals in those countries.[20]

PTL also has other types of programs on the drawing board, including an evangelical children's program to compete with Saturday morning children's shows, a youth-oriented show featuring rock and roll hits of the 1950's and a Christian soap opera with a strong emphasis on Christianity as the solution to everyday problems.

Bakker, an ordained minister and native of Muskegon, Michigan, along with his wife, Tammy Faye, traveled for eight years as evangelists in the Assembly of God Churches after he attended Bible School.

An innovator in Christian television, in 1965, he helped pioneer the successful "700 Club" for the Christian Broadcasting Network in Virginia. The first Christian talk show ever attempted. For several years, he and Tammy appeared on their own "Jim and Tammy Show," a nationally syndicated children's program produced by CBN. Leaving Virginia in 1972, Jim assisted several small Christian television stations across the country and started TBN's talk show.

In 1974, he went to Charlotte, North Carolina to help what was then a small, struggling Christian program, running on Channel 36, WRET-TV. This was the beginning of the present PTL Television Network. His vision that Christians could effectively demonstrate their way of life through television has led to the "PTL Club" and the PTL Satellite Network.[21]

In January of 1980, Bakker received the Jerusalem Award from Christians United for Israel, headed by Reverend David A. Lewis. The award is given annually to the most outstanding friend of Israel in Christian endeavor. Lewis said that receipt of the award was for outstanding loyalty and prayer support for the Jewish people on the PTL Club.[22]

PTL, like CBN and TBN, has a lease agreement with RCA on its Satcom II Satellite. Receiving and transmitting from its own earth dish, PTL is able to broadcast "live" across the face of America with Christian programming 24 hours a day.

A 60 station telephone bank plus a sophisticated diverter system is kept active 24 hours a day to handle the more than 10,000 calls that come to PTL weekly. PTL's guests range from the famous —Pat Boone, Gary Paxton, Chuck Colson, actor Dean Jones, Senator Mark Hatfield, and astronaut Jim Erwin — to people from all walks of life. All of these guests have one thing in common: they have all had a "born-again" experience with Jesus which they communicate to the viewers.

PTL follows up each person who responds to the gospel message by sending Bible correspondence courses through an in-house office of the International Correspondence Institute. In addition to this mail follow-up activity, an interdenominational group of over 3,000 local pastors around the country assist PTL's evangelistic efforts with referral, follow-up, and local church involvement.

Many television professionals say that PTL's Heritage Village facilities are among the best in the country. The network has committed itself to producing the finest quality in all of its endeavors. The studio building is a giant replica of the historic Bruton Parish Church in colonial Williamsburg. PTL's broadcast center is equipped with nearly two million dollars worth of television production and taping equipment.

PTL operates its own post office near Heritage Village in order to handle the more than 10,000 letters that come in daily. With the aid of nearly 700 dedicated staff members and the most modern computers available, each letter is carefully read and acknowledged. Every prayer request is also sent to the intercessory prayer chapel where the entire staff, in hourly shifts, intercedes for individual needs. This interaction with the PTL partners helps Bakker measure the effectiveness of his ministry. Most followers say they don't see Bakker as a spiritual "leader." They see him as their minister and feel that God is using him to direct PTL.

In the fall of 1978, Heritage Church and Missionary Fellowship, Inc. — the formal name for the PTL television network — opened its doors to the first class at Heritage Schools, offering courses in evangelism and communications. The school draws upon some of the world's most noted evangelists and communicators as guest instructors.

Students of Heritage University come from 33 states and several foreign countries. They are registered for one of twelve majors, ranging from radio/television production, music and drama, to the Bible, evangelism, Christian education, missions, journalism, photography, finite math, psychology and practical theology. The university has applied to offer associate and baccalaureate degrees in these fields.[23]

The people who are supports of the PTL efforts to win the satellite space race are much like the other two religious networks. The *Charlotte Observer* interviewed these volunteers:

Mary Hold of Mooresville, North Carolina, a PTL volunteer phone counselor and secretary for a year, kneels over prayer requests in the silence of the network's light blue intercessory prayer room where volunteers pray for others.

In the corner is a photograph of "Squeaky' Fromme, the Charles Manson follower who attempted to assassinate President Gerald Ford. She sent the picture of herself and a cellmate, asking prayer. Her request was granted.

In this room of cushiony antique sofas and chairs, all 650 staff members and 300 volunteers pray over each day's average of 600 telephone requests for salvation, blessings, healings, jobs and business successes.

People like Linda Fuller and Mary Holt are as much a part of PTL as Jim Bakker and his smooth television presentation. Twenty-seven year old Mrs. Fuller is among more than 500,000 "partners" who send monthly donations to PTL. She phones PTL's 24-hour prayer line to request prayers and blessings to relieve her burdens. Mrs. Holt is one of 300 volunteers, mostly retired, who donate time to PTL. A 52 year old housewife, Mrs. Holt is always ready to help. You don't have to know all the answers — just direct them to God, who has all the answers, she said. After praying, Mrs. Holt signs a postcard to be sent to the caller. "I prayed for you today," a short message on the card begins. It's signed, "your intercessory prayer partner, Mary."

Hill Appleford, 62, a retired vocational rehabilitation superintendent from Fort Lauderdale, Florida, moved to Charlotte four years ago to be near his children and grandchildren. "For three years, I just sat and did nothing," he said. "Life has so much meaning and more fulfillment for me now. There's so much love and compassion here. You want to live for the Lord and you want others to see Jesus through your daily life. I just wish I could express in words what is in my heart."

For others, too, PTL holds the answer to dreams and prayers. Charlotte is their Mecca.

Many come though they really can't afford the move, said representatives for the Crisis Assistance Ministry and the Travelers Aid Society. The agencies help them find food, clothing and medication. . .and give them bus tickets back home.

"We do have a lot of people who appear here and expect PTL to take care of them," said Nancy Nagglehout, director of PTL's counseling department. "People are here to do specific jobs. PTL (as an employer) is not the place for everyone.

62

Joe and Margaret Pike, volunteer phone counselors, say PTL is the place for them. At ages 64 and 62, respectively, they sold their home of 55 years in California and their cemetery plots and moved here with Mrs. Pike's 93 year old mother.

"I just wanted to do some little bit, anything to help PTL," said Mrs. Pike, already a $100-1-month partner. "I just want to help. It's a real adventure in my life but that's the way I want my life to end up — helping at PTL."

As CBN, PTL and TBN successes continue to increase, the National Christian Network and LeSea Broadcasting are also making new gains.

Lester Sumrall says that his broadcast ministry, as have many other religious broadcasters, began with a vision. In 1965 God spoke to him in Manila, Philippines and directed him to use television to win souls. His company, LeSea Broadcasting got off the ground and has grown to include three UHF television stations in Indianapolis, Miami, and South Bend, and a radio station also in South Bend. The firm produces and distributes Christian programming in over 200 cities and towns and has a television outreach with ministries in Japan, the Philippines, Canada, Iran and Columbia, South America. Most of the growth has occurred in the past five years.

The National Christian Network (NCN) is arriving on the broadcast scene in 1980 via the RCA Satcom III. The NCN approach to the marketplace is quite different from the other Christian Networks in its program distributor functioning in what it calls "a bonafide network format." NCN sales literature states that it programming will appeal to and service approximately 85% of the church groups including Catholic, Jewish, Protestant and Evangelical denominations. NCN has no vested interest in the programming. NCN boasts that it is America's authentic religious network and that it attracts a broad base of viewers not just the charismatic movement. The Satcom III Satellite is a broader communication system for all religious broadcasters.

CHAPTER VII

RELIGIOUS BROADCASTING SURVEYS

Who's viewing? How often? What do they watch? Why have they listened for nearly 60 years? Do minister's families watch more than others? These and numerous other questions have been asked about religious radio and television over the years and are still being asked today.

There are only a few published studies that have been conducted over the past 40 years to determine these questions. They are listed below. I have selected some data from each study that was of interest to me. Each of the studies is in the Appendix in the back of this book.

1. "Religion on the Air in Chicago," Everett Parker, *The Register*, Chicago Theological Seminary, January 1942.
2. "Who Listens to Religious Broadcasts Anymore?" Ronald Johnstone, *Journal of Broadcasting*, Winter 1971-72.
3. *Television-Radio Audience and Religion*, Everett Parker, David, Barry and Dallas Smythe, Harper and Brothers, New York, 1955.
4. Religious Broadcasting in Southern California, George Hill, an unpublished doctoral dissertation, City University, Los Angeles, California 1980.
5. "Will Electric Church Replace Traditional Worship?" *Emerging Trends*, Vol. 1, No. 5, May 1979, Princeton Research Center, Princeton, New Jersey.
6. "A Telephone Survey of Religious Program Preferences Among Listeners and Viewers in Los Angeles," Fred I. Casmir, *Central States Speech Journal*, Spring 1959.

The above surveys span 40 years. They were produced in Chicago, Illinois; Long Beach, California; and Los Angeles, California; and New

64

Haven, Connecticut. The Johnstone and Gallup surveys were national polls.

One of the broadest studies done of audience and religion was under the supervision of Everett C. Parker, David W. Barry and Dallas W. Smythe (1956). It was called "The Communications Research Project," which was under the supervision of Yale University Divinity School, and Liston Pope, Dean of the Divinity School. It was sponsored and largely supported by the Broadcasting and Film Commission of the National Council of Churches of Christ. Completion of the work was made possible by a grant from the Carnegie Corporation of New York. The survey was made at New Haven, Connecticut.

This is the only study relating to the viewing and listening habits of ministers and minister's families and comparing this data with the viewing habits of the general population. It is the only survey that I could find that is a complete book of studies on religious broadcasting.

The researchers interviewed the ministers of New Haven Protestant churches to determine their attitudes toward the policies and practices in religious broadcasting. Data was collected on their likes and dislikes. Also collected were the opinions of the ministers relative to the influence that religious broadcasting had on their church members. The researchers also asked the ministers and their families what kind of programs they saw on television and heard on the radio.

Do ministers watch religious broadcasts? The ministers reported that they had little time for watching television or listening to the radio. One minister said that he did not have time to watch television or listen to the radio at all. Fourteen of the 91 ministers reported that they utilized both television and radio. Twenty-eight related that they watched television but did not listen to the radio and forty-eight claimed that they restricted themselves to listening to the radio. The survey indicated that ministers and their families do not differ significantly from the general population in viewing specific programs. However, there was a significant difference in ministers and their families' habits in listening to the radio. The chart below shows the habits of the ministers and their families radio and television interests in relation to the general population.

One of the interest facts about this survey is that both minister's families and the general population rank religious programs sixth in rank of choice of television programs. On the other hand, there are more religious programs available on the radio and minister's families rank them third while the general population ranked them fifth.

It may be noted that the data indicates that there are two more places where the discrepancy of ranking involves more than one degree. It

TABLE 1
A Comparison of Radio and Television Interests

Minister's Families		All Families	
	Television		
1.	Drama	1.	Drama
2.	Sports	2.	Sports
3.	Quiz	3.	Variety
4.	Variety	4.	Quiz
5.	News	5.	News
6.	Religion	6.	Religion
7.	Music	7.	Music
8.	Other types	8.	Other types
	Radio		
1.	Music	1.	Sports
2.	News	2.	Drama
3.	Religion	3.	News
4.	Sports	4.	Music
5.	Drama	5.	Religion
6.	Quiz	6.	Quiz
7.	Variety	7.	Variety
8.	Other types	8.	News Commentators
		9.	Other types

Source: *Television-Radio Audience and Religion*, p. 83.

One of the interesting facts about this survey is that both minister's families and the general population rank religious programs sixth in rank of choice of television programs. On the other hand, there are more religious programs available on the radio and ministers' families rank them third while the general population ranked them fifth.

It may be noted that the data indicates that there are two more places where the discrepancy of ranking involves more than one degree. It may be seen from radio that the general population ranks drama second, but the minister's families rank it fifth. Music and sports are ranked in exact reverse between the two groups relative to radio. The minister's families ranked music on radio first and sports fourth; the general population ranked sports first and ranked music fourth.

66

One conclusion that may be deduced from the data is that the ministers and their families rely on radio more for direct news bulletins and opinion forming somewhat less than the general population.

Table 2 shows the order of program preference between families of ministers and the general population.

Table 2 indicates that preference of television programs are almost the same for the two groups, the ministerial families and the households of the general population. Both of the groups included 15 programs of similar influences.

It may be noted that the minister's families included two religious programs among their top fifteen on television (Bishop Sheen and This is My Life), but the general population included only one, Bishop Sheen; they ranked it higher (6th) than did minister's families (8th).

Who Listens to Religious Broadcasting Anymore?

Another study on the influence of religious broadcasting was undertaken by Dr. Ronald L. Johnstone while he was the director of research for the Lutheran Council in the United States of America. It is the only broad-based national study done in the past 10 years. The goal of the survey was to determine the influence of religious radio programs generally and how much influence, if any, the Lutheran Hour exerted among listeners. This was also the most recent national study that dealt only with religious radio.

The data in Table 3 indicates that those who listen occasionally and those who almost never listen have about the same number of people. The author thought that it was a significant finding to find that almost half of the people who are adults in the United States listen to a religious radio program — at least occasionally. The proportion turned out to be 48 percent.

The findings of Dr. Johnstone's study are similar to the study done by Fred Casmir in 1957. Casmir conducted his study in Los Angeles. He found that 24% of the people never listen as compared with 24% in Johnstone's sample. He found that 24% did listen as compared to 2% of Johnstone's study.

Even in light of the fact that Casmir's data came from one metropolitan area and relied upon telephone interviews, the similarities between the two studies suggest that there has not been a significant shift in the religious broadcasting audience since 1957.

Several demographic variables were examined relative to those who listen to religious broadcasting in Johnstone's study; namely, age, sex, denominational affiliation, educational level, geographic region, degree of

67

TABLE 2
Preference of Programs between the general population
and ministers families

Minister's families	All families

Television

	Minister's families		All families
1.	John Cameron Swazey	1.	John Cameron Swazey
2.	Studio One	2.	I Love Lucy
3.	Voice of Firestone	3.	Studio One
4.	Arthur Godfrey	4.	Philco Playhouse
5.	Strike It Rich	5.	Milton Berle
6.	I Love Lucy	6.	Fulton J. Sheen
7.	Toast of the Town	7.	Arthur Godfrey
8.	Fulton J. Sheen	8.	Strike It Rich
9.	Your Show of Shows	9.	Voice of Firestone
10.	This is the Life	10.	Groucho Marx
11.	Philco Playhouse	11.	Suspense
12.	Fred Waring	12.	Your Show of Shows
13.	Kate Smith Show	13.	Toast of the Town
14.	Lux Video Theatre	14.	Cogate Comedy Hour
15.	Mama	15.	Lux Video Theatre

Radio

	Minister's families		All families
1.	Metropolitan Opera	1.	The Catholic Hour
2.	NBC Symphony	2.	Arthur Godfrey
3.	Longine Symphonette	3.	Strike It Rich
4.	New York Philharmonic Symp.	4.	Groucho Marx
5.	WELI Morning News	5.	Telephone Hour
6.	Twenty Questions	6.	Voice of Firestone
7.	Lowell Thomas	7.	The Greatest Story Ever Told
8.	The Lutheran Hour	8.	Jack Benny
9.	Telephone Hour	9.	Twenty Questions
10.	Eversong	10.	Lux Radio Theatre
11.	Railroad Hour	11.	Break the Bank
12.	Jack Benny	12.	Railroad Hour
13.	National Radio Pulpit	13.	Lowell Thomas tied with
14.	Old Fashioned Revival Hour	13.	Fulton Lewis, Jr.
15.	Gabriel Heatter	14.	My True Story

TABLE 3

(Frequency of Listening to Religious Radio Programs
Proportion and Number of U. S. Adult Population)

Frequency	Number	Proportion
Often	303	20%
Occasionally	418	28%
Seldom	393	26%
Never	376	25%
Not Ascertained	4	0%
TOTALS	1,490	99%

religious commitment and interest, frequency of attendance at religious services and urban/rural residence.

Denominational Affiliations

By examining the data in Table 4, it becomes apparent that Protestants are more likely to listen to religious radio broadcasts than any other religious group. The findings are similar to those found by Casmir. (67% Protestant and 42% Catholic regular and occasional listeners compared with 57% Protestant and 33% Catholic frequent and occasional listeners in the sample.) The findings indicated that Jews and those who are not religious are least likely to listen to religious broadcasting. Of importance is the fact that the Catholic audience was barely ahead of the Jewish and non-religious listeners. Perhaps this is why most of the religious programs are produced by Protestants.

Frequency of Attendance at Religious Services

The data in Table 4 indicates that those who attend church the most are the most likely to listen to religious broadcasting. There is a very strong correlation between frequency of church attendance and frequency of listening to religious radio programs.

TABLE 4
Frequency of Listening to Religious Radio Programs by Various Characteristics of Respondents

A. Religious or Denominational Preference	Often	Occasionally	Seldom	Never	NA	Total
Protestant	26%	31%	25%	18%		976
Baptist	37%	31%	20%	13%		333
Episcopal	13%	22%	28%	38%		32
Lutheran	13%	34%	32%	22%		120
Methodist	18%	34%	33%	15%		187
Presbyterian	19%	30%	32%	31%	1	67
United Church of Christ	24%	29%	19%	22%		51
Other Protestants	30%	25%	26%	17%	1	156
Catholic	8%	17%	30%	37%		355
Jew	13%	17%	25%	46%		24
Other	26%	16%	24%	33%		42
None	11%	18%	27%	45%		93
B. Age						
18-29	11%	16%	31%	42%		329
30-39	17%	22%	31%	30%		246
40-49	22%	30%	25%	23%		247
50-59	23%	36%	22%	19%		235
60-69	27%	30%	28%	16%		217
70+	27%	43%	18%	12%		181
C. Geographic Region of Residence						
Northeast	13%	28%	24%	35%		357
Midwest	18%	29%	29%	23%		419
Southeast	30%	33%	21%	16%		213
South	34%	28%	24%	14%		258
Mountain & Pacific	13%	23%	31%	33%	1	243
D. Urban/Rural Residence						
Large Metropolitan	15%	22%	24%	39%	1	330
Small Metropolitan	21%	28%	26%	25%		615
Non-metropolitan (town)	20%	36%	28%	16%		233
Non-metropolitan (rural)	26%	30%	28%	16%		312

Age of Respondents

Table 4 provides evidence that there is a positive correlationship between the age of the individual and the frequency that he listens to religious radio programs. If the "often" category is combined with the "occasional" category, there is a range of 28% for the youngest respondents who are between 18-29 years of age, to 70% for the oldest respondents with an age range above 70 years old. There are several explanations for this dramatic change in the various age ranges. For example, older persons tend to stay home more than younger people. They also have established strong radio listening habits in the years before television came into commercial operation. They have more interest in traditional religious forms, which is characteristic of radio religious broadcasting. Thus, the relationship between age and frequency of listening to religious broadcasting on radio was found by the researcher to be significant.

Sex of Respondents

Table 4 indicates that sex does not show a difference in the frequency of listening to religious radio programs as far as males or females are concerned. It has been thought that women are more involved in religious activities than men are but this did not occur in this study.

Education

The researcher assumed that the more formal education a person had the less likely that person was to be involved in listening to religious broadcasting. The data in Table 4 supports this presupposition. It may be observed that as the educational level of the respondents increases, their numbers decrease relative to listening to religious broadcasting. The only exception is in the highest educational category where 21% reported that they often turn on the radio to listen to religious broadcasting. It may be observed that this discrepancy essentially disappears when the categories of "often" and "occasionally" are combined. The proportions then show a direct regression from the lowest to the highest educational category:

1.	62%
2.	54%
3.	43%
4.	39%
5.	37%
6.	31%

Geographic Region

The author assumed that most of the religious audience would be in the Midwest and the South because a large number of Protestants are concentrated in these regions, especially Baptists. It may be noted by observing Table 4 that this expectation materializes. The data in Table 4 clearly supports this conceptualization. The highest frequency is in the South and next, the residents of the Midwest. They exceed the frequency of listening to religious radio broadcasts by individuals living in the Northeastern, Pacific and Mountain states. The researcher believed that different denominational concentration was the essential difference.

Urban/Rural Difference

The data in Table 4 indicates that the further a person lives from an urban center, the more likely he is to listen to a religious radio program. This is continuous in progression if the two categories of "often" and "occasional" are combined.

Conclusions — Johnstone Survey

There are several conclusions that may be drawn from this study. There is a combination of factors that contribute significantly to the possibility of a person listening to radio religious broadcasting. The composite picture would consist of an older person of either sex who probably lives in a southern state and in a rural area, with relatively little education, a member of a Protestant religion, who attends church regularly and believes that religion is an important aspect of his life. In other words, religious radio broadcasts probably will not reach the non-Christian or minimally committed Christian, the young, the highly educated and those who live in the city.

A Telephone Survey of Religious Program Preferences

Casmir's study presented several other significant findings. His sample consisted of 349 Protestants, 128 Catholics and 17 Jews. The results indicated that almost half of the people taking part in the sample watched religious programs and/or listened to them on radio.

Casmir found that Protestants spent 2 hours and 14 minutes week watching or listening to religious broadcasting. Catholics spent 1 hour and 10 minutes, Jews 1 hour and 4 minutes.

The three religious groups in the survey preferred Sunday as the most important day of the week to be exposed to religious broadcasting, indicating 46 percent of the Protestants, 47.3 percent of the Catholics, and 52.9 percent of the Jews.

One of the areas of Casmir's study which had not been done before pertained to listening and viewing as it was related to church attendance. Regular Protestant churchgoers listened to religious radio more regularly than Catholics or Jews. Regular Protestant television viewers were also the most frequency churchgoers.

The largest group listening to religious programs on radio were those who listen sometimes (35.6%), while 24.2% listen regularly, and almost the same percentage never listen to religious programs on radio (24.3%). Also, the largest percentage of those viewing religious programs were those who view sometimes (31.2%). There were a few percent more who regularly view (26.1%) than who never view (20.3%).

Religion in Chicago

Everett C. Parker conducted a study in 1940 to find out if the people of Chicago listen to more religious broadcasting that originates from outside the city or whether they listen more to religious broadcasting that comes from within the city. He also wanted to find out if most of the programs from radio studios were from churches in the area.

To obtain the data, he conducted interviews with representatives of the radio stations' management. He also asked the same questions of the sponsors of the religious programs. The stations in Chicago from which he obtained his information were WAAF, WAIT, WBBM, WCFL, WCRW, WEDC, WENR, WDES, WGN, WHFC, WHIP, WIND, WJJD, WLS, WMAQ, WMBI and WSBC.

Parker found that 46 hours a week were used for religious broadcasting by Chicago's commercial radio stations. There were 77 different religious programs involved in that time span which took up 2.9 percent of the total broadcast time of these stations.

The researcher found that of the 77 religious programs, 14 were interdenominational, 41 were Protestant, 11 were Roman Catholic, 1 was Jewish, 2 were Christian Science, and 8 of the programs did not have a denominational affiliation.

The researcher said that it was difficult to determine the size of the radio audience of the religious programs that were on the air in Chicago. He noted that certain factors indicated that the audience was relatively large.

TABLE 5
Church Attendance and Radio Listening

Faith	Listen Regularly	Listen Some	Listen Seldom	Never	TOTAL
		Regular Churchgoers			
Protestant	(60) 31.4%	(91) 47.7%	(21) 11.0%	(9) 9%	(191)
Catholic	(12) 12.9%	(23) 24.7%	(16) 17.2%	(42) 45.2%	(93)
Jewish	0	(2) 50.0%	(2) 50.0%	0	(4)
		Occasional Churchgoers			
Protestant	(26) 23.9%	(37) 33.9%	(24) 22.0%	(22) 20.2%	(109)
Catholic	(10) 37.1%	(6) 22.2%	(3) 11.1%	(8) 29.6%	(27)
Jewish	0	(5) 41.7%	(3) 25%	(4) 33.3%	(12)
		Non-Churchgoers			
Protestant	(11) 22.5%	(8) 16.3%	(10) 20.4%	(20) 40.8%	(49)
Catholic	0	(3) 37.5%	0	(5) 62.5%	(8)
Jewish	0	(1) 100%	0	0	(1)
		TOTALS			
349 Protestants:	(97) 27.8%	(136) 38.9%	(55) 15.8%	(61) 17.5%	
128 Catholics:	(22) 17.2%	(32) 25.0%	(19) 24.8%	(55) 43.0%	
17 Jews:	0	(8) 47.1%	(5) 29.4%	(4) 23.5%	
494 TOTAL:	(119) 24.2%	(176) 35.6%	(79) 15.9%	(120) 24.3%	

TABLE 6
Church Attendance and TV Viewing

Faith	View Regularly	View Some	View Seldom	View Never	TOTALS
			Regular Churchgoers		
Protestant	(61) 31.9%	(67) 35.1%	(34) 17.8%	(29) 15.2%	(191) 54.6%
Catholic	(26) 28.0%	(29) 31.1%	(16) 17.2%	(22) 22.7%	(93) 72.7%
Jewish	0	(1) 25.0%	(2) 50.0%	(1) 25.0%	(4) 23.5%
			Occasional Churchgoers		
Protestant	(21) 19.2%	(35) 32.1%	(26) 23.9%	(27) 24.8%	(100) 31.1%
Catholic	(9) 33.3%	(6) 22.3%	(4) 14.8%	(8) 29.6%	(27) 21.1%
Jewish	(3) 25.0%	(1) 8.3%	(8) 66.7%	0	(12) 70.6%
			Non-Churchgoers		
Protestant	(7) 14.3%	(12) 24.5%	(19) 38.8%	(11) 22.4%	(49) 14.4%
Catholic	(2) 12.5%	(3) 37.5%	(2) 25.0%	(2) 25.0%	(8) 6.2%
Jewish	(1) 100%	0	0	0	(1) 5.9%

TOTALS

349 Protestants:

(89) 25.5%   (114) 23.7%   (79) 22.6%   (67) 19.2%

128 Catholics:

(36) 28.1%   (38) 29.7%   (22) 17.2%   (32) 25.0%

17 Jews:

(4) 23.5%   (2) 11.8%   (10) 58.8%   (1) 5.9%

494 TOTAL:

(129) 26.1%   (154) 31.2%   (111) 22.4%   (100) 20.3%

75

He listed them as follows:

1. 49 programs were sponsored by commercial interests;
2. 18 originate in place that require rental of the equipment or part of the equipment that was used;
3. 33 of the programs relied on money sent in by the listeners to pay radio fees and other costs for airing the programs; and
4. several of the religious programs had a very large mail response.

Conclusions — Parker Survey

Parker came to the following conclusions concerning his study of religious broadcasting in Chicago. He felt that the programs had too much "talk" involved. He meant by this that most of the programs centered around a sermon, or around a regular church service with a sermon involved.

Parker found that many of the programs were of poor quality and that their value as religious programs was doubtful. Many of the ministers attempted to take advantage of the audience's superstitions and sentimentality. The appeals for money were blatant; yet they must have been effective enough to pay for the radio time and even bring a profit to the minister in charge.

It was Parker's opinion that the network programs of the National Broadcasting Company and the Columbia Broadcasting System were of a much higher quality generally speaking than the average program. He was especially delighted with NBC's National Vespers with Harry Emerson Fordick as preacher. He liked CBS's Wings over Jordan and The Church of the Air. Parker found out that not all of the programs were available to the different stations. For example, Dr. Fordick was often crowded out of a spot on Sunday in Chicago because of professional football.

Mr. Parker states that too many of the network programs come from New York. While this might be a good method of the New York ministers to let people know what they were thinking, it would probably be better if the audience could hear the thinking of ministers from different geographic locations in the United States. Mr. Parker felt that it might be a good idea for New York also.

Recommendations — Parker Survey

The following recommendations were made by Parker to improve

76

the quality of religious broadcasting in Chicago. He thought that there should be less "talk" and more religious music on the programs. He noted that the greatest composers in the world have devoted their talents to the writing of religious music but there was not a single program which presented the music of these masters in the area of religious themes.

The author felt that the churches needed to study how to provide programs to best suit the particular facilities of the radio ministry. He noted that the "Town Meeting to the Air," the "Music Appreciation Hour," and the "American School of the Air," did as much in the field of secular education.

The author suggested that religious broadcasting include such things as round table discussions, forums and quiz techniques.

Parker readily admitted to the fact that radio broadcasting was expensive and that the programs he suggested probably were beyond the means of the local church but their production could be done by national denominations and interdenominational agencies.

Unchurch American and Religious Broadcasting

In 1977, the Gallup organization's Princeton Religion Research Center and a coalition of 30 religious groups conducted a survey on unchurched Americans. The study indicated that 28 percent of these people listened to or watched radio and television programs produced by religious organizations. Six out of ten interviewed in the overall survey were not exposed to a religious broadcasting program.

The following tables indicate the type of program seen as well as some of the specific programs that the respondents viewed.

The basis of the responses for Table 8 was, "Do you remember the names of the programs or the sponsoring groups? What were they?" This was asked only of unchurched respondents who had listened to or watched a religious program in the 30 days prior to the time of the survey.

Religious Broadcasting in Southern California

I prepared a religious broadcasting survey in the latter part of 1979 regarding such influence on the general population as a part of the research I did for my dissertation at City University Los Angeles.

A total of 372 people were surveyed relative to religious broadcasting. Of the 372 respondents, 208 were from the City of Los Angeles area and 164 were from the City of Long Beach.

TABLE 7
Type of Program

Broadcasts of religious services	55%
Testimonial or Crusade program	33%
Religious talk show	19%
Documentaries about actual people or events	19%
Dramatizations about the Bible	16%
Short spot messages	13%
Special holiday programs	11%
Animated cartoons	4%
Other	7%
Don't know/no answer	3%
TOTAL**	**183%**

**Total is more than 100% due to multiple responses.

TABLE 8
Specific Programs

Oral Roberts	12%
Billy Graham	11%
Rex Humbard	4%
P.T.L.	3%
Sponsored by the Baptists	3%
700 Club	3%
Dr. Robert Schuller	3%
Lutheran Church sponsors	1%
Garner Ted Armstrong	1%
Larry Black	1%
Holocaust	1%
Only gave call numbers	2%
Other	2%
Don't know/no answer	53%
Other	19%
TOTAL**	**117%**

**Total is more than 100% due to multiple responses.

The sample group was broken down by its demographic variables. Racially speaking, 66 were Black, 108 were White, 18 were Latin and 12 were Asian. One hundred four of the respondents were under the age of 45 and 99 were over the age of 45. From an educational perspective, 37 finished elementary school, 93 finished high school, 49 went to college, and 14 had enrolled in graduate school. Examining the respondents and classifying them by income, it was found that 106 earned more than $15,000 a year and 97 earned less than $15,000 a year. The number of males involved in the study was 101 and the number of females was 112.

The study indicated that out of 208 people in Los Angeles, 105 watched or listened to religious broadcasting while 103 did not listen. The findings indicated that 98 out of 164 people from the City of Long Beach area watched or listened to religious broadcasting.

Twenty-eight of the respondents from the Los Angeles area indicated that they sent money to religious programs which broadcast on the air, and 31 sent in money from the Long Beach area. Eighteen of the respondents from Los Angeles indicated that they attended meetings which were advertised on a religious broadcast and 21 attended from Long Beach. Ninety-five of the respondents said that they listened or saw a religious program on Sunday on radio or television while 90 from Long Beach replied in the same manner. Twenty-four of the respondents said they hear or watch religious broadcasts during the week and 32 said the same from Long Beach. Sixteen respondents said they knew of cases where people were saved by religious broadcasts and 9 from Long Beach indicated that they had known such event to occur. Twenty-one respondents from the Los Angeles area indicated that they knew of at least one person who was motivated to give up a bad habit such as smoking or drinking by listening to a religious broadcast. Fifteen from Long Beach said that they knew of such an event happening.

When do people listen/view religious broadcasts? The two tables, 9 and 10, indicate that Sunday is definitely the day. This adds some fuel to the controversy that people may be visiting the electric church instead of the local church. It should be noted that the Casmir study also indicated that most people listen/view on Sunday.

Conclusions — Hill Study

Based on the findings of the study that I made in Southern California concerning religious broadcasting, the following conclusions were made:

TABLE 9
Do you watch or listen to religious broadcasting on Sunday?

	Responses	
	Yes*	No
Los Angeles Group	90%	10%
Long Beach Group	92%	8%

*Total exceeds 100% because of overlap of those who listen/view on Sundays and weekdays.

TABLE 10
Do you watch or listen to religious broadcasting on weekdays?

	Responses	
	Yes*	No
Los Angeles Group	23%	77%
Long Beach Group	33%	67%

*Total exceed 100% because of overlap of those who listen/view on Sundays and weekdays.

1. Over 50 percent of the respondents involved in the study indicated that they watch or listen to religious broadcasting.
2. The people that live in Long Beach and those that live in Los Angeles do not differ significantly in their viewing habits of religious broadcasting. Southern Californians must be a homogeneous grouping.
3. The two groups did not differ significantly in their frequency of contributions to religious programs.
4. More respondents from both groups preferred television.
5. Most of the respondents from the two areas said that they did not know of anyone giving up a bad habit from listening or hearing religious broadcasting.
6. Approximately half of the respondents from Long Beach and Los Angeles felt that the people who participate in religious

broadcasting are sincere.

7. Most of the respondents said that they did not know of any-
    one being "saved" by listening to religious broadcasting.

Have Things Changed? — Not Much

Even with the variables of time and geographical distance, there are some interesting comparisons that can be made with the various studies. In Parker's survey, he recommended 38 years ago that there be less talk and more music. Still today, the airways to the soul overflow with preaching and sermon-oriented broadcasts with most ministers talking for the full broadcast time. However, there has been some change in that there are some stations which bring the various forms of gospel music (soul, southern gospel, inspirational, contemporary) to the public. Of course, there are just a handful of these stations now but the public is tired of being preached at. So there will be more gospel music stations. There is even a magazine, *Contemporary Religious Music*, which shares the most up-to-date information in the gospel music world each month.

To Blacks, Music Is Important

Black people have included music in their broadcasts because music has always been a vital part of the worship service, especially in Baptist, Methodist, and Pentecostal services. Parker cited four Black-oriented programs in his 1942 study. They were "Wings Over Jordan" on WVVB, a CBS network program; "Southernnaires" on WCFL, an NBC network program; "Negro Spirituals" on WSBC; and "Gospel and Spiritual Hour" on WEDC. Of the 77 programs listed by Parker, the four Black ones were music-oriented. Today, two of the five most popular black ministers on television are singers who include a lot of music in their telecast.

The overwhelming success of the "Tonight Show" type programs, the 700 Club of CBN, PTL Club of PTL and TBN's "Praise the Lord" show also illustrates the need for something other than preaching, as Parker cited.

The popularity of my programs, "Ecumenical Insights," and "Inter-Faith Forum," and KNBC-TV's "Odyssey," all of which are interview programs on religions, further illustrates Parker's point. He also recommended that drama, forums, round-table discussions and quizzes be used by religious agencies as an alternative to preaching and sermon-type programs. Only a few agencies such as The Southern Baptist, Francis Center and United Church of Christ have created excellent programs that are not of the preaching variety.

With hundreds of religious shows airing today, we see that the Christian Church has not made much progress in broadcasting since Parker made his recommendation in 1942. Parker's suggestions, however, did not fall on deaf ears in the 1940's. He wrote in the *Register* (Chicago Theological Seminary), the article "Radio Report Card." He said that based on the recommendations in his survey, the Seminary had begun producing several programs of the non-talking type. They were "Men of Power," a dramatization of the lives of great men; "Great Religious Music," performed by the Seminary Choir, and "The Bible for Today." These programs attempted to offer an alternative.

The Casmir, Johnstone, and Hill studies tend to indicate that percentages of people listening or viewing religious broadcasting have contributed to some interesting changes and challenges over the past twenty years.

Johnstone said that 48% of the adults in the United States listen to religious radio at least occasionally. Hill's study indicates 71% for TV and 86% for radio. There could be some overlapping of television viewers and radio listeners in the Casmir and Hill surveys. The big difference in the television and the radio percentage is possibly due to the vast mobility of Californians portability of radio which can be taken anywhere. According to the Southern California Broadcasters Association, there is a very high percentage of cars with radios and there is very little rapid transit in the area, which indicates that there are a lot of cars there. Additionally, there are 13 stations in Southern California and over two and a half dozen over stations broadcasting some religious programs. So the message is definitely always on the airwaves to the soul.

It must be noted in the Casmir study the reasons for listening and viewing religious programs. The choices were: (1) because of the speakers, (2) subject, and (3) music. In each sample of Protestants, Catholics and Jews, the percentage of subject choices was greater than the percentage of speaker choices. If one were to add together the percentages of "the subject" and "music," the response would greatly outweigh the percentage of those who listened or viewed because of the speaker. Perhaps this does illustrate again that when offered a choice, people will choose something other than preaching.

More Watch Television

It appears that the cathode church is viewed in much greater frequency than radio listening. The Casmir and Hill surveys tend to illustrate this. The Gallup survey also indicates some findings in that direction.

The Casmir's study of the late 1950's revealed that more Protestants and Jews preferred television. However, the Catholics in the Casmir study preferred radio nearly seven to one (45.4%), while 6.2% preferred television. It should be noted that this was during the time that Fulton Sheen, a Catholic Bishop, was quite popular on television.

The Parker study showed that minister's families and all other families ranked Sheen's program in the top eight of preferred television programs. The Hill study, done more than 20 years later, revealed that 85% of those interviewed watched TV, while only 22 listened to radio.

The Gallup survey of the unchurched in 1979 asked people to name programs listened to or watched in the past thirty days. The interviewers named television programs — The 700 Club, P.T.L., Robert Schuller, Oral Roberts, Billy Graham, Rex Humbard and Holocaust. Some of the programs may have been on radio but the survey did not indicate this.

Has religious broadcasting caused its viewers and listeners to become more ecumenical and more tolerant of other people's religious beliefs? Perhaps! In 1928, NBC's Religious Advisory Council was established. This council arrived at a statement of principles, two of which were:

1.   Religious broadcasting should be non-denominational.
2.   It should avoid matters of doctrine and controversial subjects.

The non-doctrinal and non-denominational approach that has been fostered over the past 58 years, I believe, has greatly influenced our attitudes. The Gallup publication, *Emerging Trends*, September 1979, states that one of the most dramatic trends in the 44 year history of the Gallup Poll has been a growth of religious tolerance. In 1952, when Protestants were asked if they had any experiences that made them dislike Catholics, 9% said "yes;" in 1979, only 2% gave the same response. As for Protestants disliking Jews, the response went from 8% to 2%. The Catholic response concerning Jews shifted from 6% who said they had an unpleasant experience to 2% in 1979. Catholic tolerance of Protestants went from 4% to 1%. In the poll, Jews were not asked about their experience with Protestants or Catholics.

In April, 1977, *Redbook* published a survey of 65,000 women in which they asked them how religion affects health, happiness, sex and politics. The survey indicated that women are more tolerant of people in other religions. The results were as follows:

Eight in ten women say that if a person belongs to a different religion, they still have the same chance for grace and salvation. The majority does not think the world would be a better place if everyone belonged to the same religion. Less than half in the survey felt it important for a child to learn about other religions and then make a personal choice.

The survey indicates that people are more tolerant of other religious beliefs. I suggest that the non-controversial, non-denominational approach which religious broadcasts have fostered has influenced this tolerance and has contributed to its constancy.

The Casmir, Johnstone, and Hill studies tend to indicate that the percentage of people listening or viewing a religious broadcast has remained constant. Johnstone said that 48% of the adults in the United States listen to religious broadcasts at least occasionally. The findings in the Casmir study indicated that 24% of the respondents listened regularly. Johnstone's study showed that 20% of the people listened "often." This suggests that there had been no significant shift in the proportions of persons listening between 1957 and 1970. The Hill study showed that 77 of the 372 (20%) of the respondents said that they watched religious television often. Things really haven't changed that much over the past 20 years.

CHAPTER VIII

PAY VS FREE TIME RELIGIOUS BROADCASTING

Religious radio and televison is one of the fastest growing sectors in communications according to the *New York Times*! Today, television viewers can see everything from ministers bantering social issues and parishioners healed of afflications to gala talent shows in the name of religion. Conceivably, it is a growing industry with no end in sight.

Although the networks give an estimated $3 million in air time and production costs per week to religious programming as a public service, it is the fundamentalist-oriented who pay millions to produce and air shows. Each week about 70 religious series are syndicated nationally, with groups of specials, live revival meetings and crusades sprinkled here and there on prime time television. An estimated $500 million a year is spent by ministers for the purchase of broadcast time.[1]

Some of the questions raised by critics of video evangelism and positive points are detailed in this chapter.

"Most of these people are on television to make money so they can expand their television exposure and make more money. . .they don't do anything else," said Dr. Everett Parker, Director of the Office of Communications for the United Church of Christ. "The major Protestant faiths spend about as much a year on food relief in India, Africa and South America as does one evangelist buying TV time. He doesn't spend any money on food relief. He doesn't spend any money to help anybody."

Of course, this has always been the rhetoric of those spreading a "social gospel," answer the evangelists. To the evangelist, feeding the belly comes secondary to saving the soul.

"To us, the whole point in having a TV program is to reach men, women and children with the knowledge that Jesus Christ died for them," says Paul Calentine, former manager of KHOF-TV's King Productions.

"Jesus died and paid the cost of our salvation so if just one person is reached with the dollars we spend, we consider it worth the price," he says.

Most other TV evangelists would probably agree with him. "Of course," he adds, "we know it's difficult to talk to someone who is hungry; we understand that. But there are plenty of organizations dedicated to feeding the hungry. Each organization has a different calling. You do something different than I do. So I can't see the conflict. We feed the soul, they feed the body."

Still, some evangelism-geared media experts disagree with this approach in spreading the gospel. Because of the expense-versus-the-coverage idea, spot messages, they claim, are more functional.

The concept, however, is not a new one. The United Presbyterian Church pioneered the TV spot idea in 1966 with a "God is Alive" film rebutting the then current "God is Dead" theory. Since then, many church organizations turned to the spot message. Five or six spots can be turned out for what a typical half-hour film costs. And they were being dropped into unusual places.

The Episcopalians, for example, had their spot placed during the middle of a televised ballgame. It showed a viewer watching television where early Christians faced lions in an arena. The tag line stated: "Being a Christian didn't used to be a spectator sport. It still isn't."

Yet most of the spot messages used were of the moral-ethical-social blend as opposed to the go-to-church or salvation message. Unfortunately, few of them are ever long enough to determine a result.

Until recently, the National Council of Churches (NCC) took no official stance on TV evangelism but does hold to a philosophy of staying away from "selling the faith," especially to those who believe they have already bought the goods.

Now the NCC and other mainstream established groups, including the Southern Baptists, the Roman Catholic Church and some Jewish groups, are questioning the boom in religious broadcasting to the point of rivalry, according to the *New York Times*.[2]

"Established" churches have several gripes with paid broadcasters. They suspect that the electric church is draining away members and garnering dollars that might otherwise go into church collection plates. They say that this is especially true among older people.

In January 1980, several top mainline Protestant and Catholic communicators, who rely on free time on Sunday mornings, met in New York City for a symposium on the electric church, its fundamentalist preachers, and its perceived threat to liberal and moderate Christianity. Speaking at the conference, Robert Liebert, a psychologist at the State University of New York, contended that the conflict is a "holy war" between the conven-

tional church and "airwave evangelism" with nothing less than the defini-
tion of Christianity at stake.[3]

"Pitchmen" is the name given to electric church preachers by Lutheran minister and University of Chicago Professor, Martin Marty. "They
raise money but fail to winnow any commitment from their far-flung audience. If not the enemy, then at least they are a rival. The loser is the local
church," says Marty.[4]

Television minister, Robert Schuller of Garden Gover, California,
strongly disagrees with Liebert and the "they-against-us" attitude suggested.
He disagrees with the term "electric church" and says that he himself is
from an "established" church, the Reform Church of America. Religious
News Service quotes Schuller as saying that his weekly television program
"Hour of Power," is "not a church and I'm the first to say that."

In an article in *Christianity Today*, CBN's marketing specialist John
Roos rebutted the argument that TV preachers weaken the local church.
He said that in CBN audience surveys, 34 percent of CBN viewers say that
they have become more involved in the local church as a result of watching
CBN. Only 2 percent say they have gotten less involved through watching
CBN, according to Roos. He added that CBN reaches 350,000 households
daily; 65 percent of the viewers are women; average age is 49; and 15 percent are Baptist; and Roman Catholics and Assemblies of God each comprise 11 percent of the audience.[5]

Religion writer Russell Chandler noted in a recent Los Angeles
Times article that there is no hard evidence that the electric churches are
emptying pews and congregational coffers.

Ben Armstrong, former Presbyterian pastor and executive director,
National Religious Broadcasters, says that the NRB has won. Stations are
just not picking up their programs such as Lamp Unto Your Feet, "that
are more like the government-controlled programs in the European sense.
People are much more willing to watch and listen to our kind (fundamentalist) of program and pay for them."

"During the past several years, local stations have been increasingly
unwilling to provide free religious programming when they can get paid for
it," says William Fore, communications secretary for the National Council
of Churches in Christ.

Programs such as CBS's "Lamp," and "Look Up and Live"have
dropped from 127 broadcasts in 1971 to 92 in 1980.   In an analysis of
Arbitron survey (the rating service for radio as Nielsen is for television), the
communications staff of the United Church of Christ acknowledged that
"while approximately equal numbers of paid and non-paid religious pro-

grams were carried in 1959, by 1978, non-paid programs had dropped to eight percent of the total."[6]

Armstrong says that nothing makes viewers sit at home and watch programs or contribute to programs. When a program goes out over the airwaves, it is there for everyone. He adds, "Broadcasting is shifting power from the clergy to the layman with his hand on the dial."

In a *Ministry* magazine article, Fore asked this question: "Is religious broadcasting creating an electronic church that substitutes an anonymous and undemanding commitment for the personal involvement of the local congregation?" He provided a synopsis of how the average American spends his time during the week. He notes that the average person spends 53 hours sleeping, 26 hours working and 8 hours eating. Of 57 hours spent in leisure activities each week, 26.4 hours find Mr. and Mrs. Average American in front of the TV. Radio receives 21.3 hours; newspapers, 4.2 hours; magazines, 3.3 hours; with records and tapes rounded out to 1.3 hours. Attending movies, sports or cultural events occupies only 17 minutes of our average American's week, while reading books trails the list with 12 minutes. All other activities fit into the remaining 24 hours. One can observe by these statistics that the average American spends more time listening to radio and watching TV combined than any other activity in his life except sleeping. He spends an average of 47.7 hours a week watching television and listening to the radio.[7]

Fore added that he wasn't worried so much about the big business aspect of the electronic church although he felt that the big business aspect of the electronic church should worry the people who are engaged in it. He noted that "What worries me about all this activity is not the financial successes nor the big business aspects of this evangelism—although I suspect it should worry them. What worries me is whether this electronic church is in fact pulling people away from the local church. It is substituting an anonymous (and therefore undemanding) commitment that is the essence of the local church."

Fore pointed out that even the most naive observer soon discovers that it is relatively easy to raise funds by religious broadcasting on radio and television but it's almost impossible to re-funnel part of these funds back into the local community. Fore included an observation in the article concerning the electronic church by Martin Marty.

Marty described this competition between the electronic and the local church this way. "Late Staurday night, Mr. and Mrs. Invisible Religion get their jollies from the ruffled-shirted, pink-tuxedoed men and the high-coiffeured, low-necklined celebrity women who talk about themselves under the guise of born-again autobiographies. Sunday mornings the watchers get their jollies as Holy Ghost entertainers caressing microphones among spurting fountains as a highly professional, charismatic (in two senses) leader entertains them."[8]

"Are they to turn off that very set and then make their way down the block to a congregation of real believers, sinners, offkey choirs, sweaty and homely people who need them, people they do not like but are supposed to love, ordinary pastors who preach grace along with calls to discipleship, pleas for stewardship that do not come well-oiled? Never. Well, hardly ever."

In his personal newsletter entitled, *Context*, Marty wrote, "The ultimate effect of the electronic church. . .is to turn people loose on a world of things, offering even more things. They motivate sales people to sell more, the greedy to get more, the followers to consume more and possess more of the world. They parade the successful."

In a ringing conclusion to his article, Fore said that he did not believe that an evangelizing program could be successful by propagating the gospel through the electronic church. He said that the community church has to do more to help some of the 61 million "unchurched" Americans, many of whom have deep religious convictions, to consider at least the possibility that the local church can satisfy some of their needs.

He added that the local church could show how God works in the lives of people through comedy, entertainment and discussion and documentary. He said that the local church can develop programs that will encourage religious discussion in the car pool, at the office or in the church.

Finally, he warned "We will have to resist being taken over, and taken in, by the power of the media and its cultural biases. We will have to resist the temptation to try to be the gospel in the mass media, to be an electronic church, which pulls people away from the real local church, that place where the people of God find the strength, the guidance, and the courage to persevere in the faith that God is in Jesus Christ. No amount of 'success' whether measured in millions of dollars or even in millions of persons reached is worth that."[9]

Of course, the controversy between the broadcast religionist and the local church is nothing new for the 70's and 80's. It has been a topic of much discussion since the 1920's.

In an article published in *Literary Digest* in 1927, it was said by Quin A. Ryan that "religion has got radio and radio has got religion" and religious radio was a divine blessing. Apparently Ryan was in favor of religious radio. The article also stated:

Religious broadcasting has been so successful that there has been predictions of 'radio churches' to supplant poorly equipped rural pastorates. A community chapel would replace the little red meeting house and a radio horn replace the little red preacher.

One writer in a religious publication foretells the passing of the circuit-riding parson, the wheezy organ, the homemade choir, the inept sermons and sparse attendance. The pastor, he predicts, will become instead a social organizer and superintendent of the radio services. The congregation will gather to hear the sermon of a famous metropolitan divine and will join with the singing of renowned artists miles away.

The opposing debaters in the article contended that people will never be satisfied with merely auricular attendance in church; that religion is more than simple hearing—whatever the belief. They also argued that services on the radio lose their devotedness; that the churchgoer misses the warmth and comfort of personal attendance; that there is lacking the communal spirit and the sense of holiness. People have been saying the same things about the electric church for 50 years.

In an editorial in *Literary Digest* in 1928, it was noted that the religious broadcasting programs will cause the small church preacher to lose his congregation because people tend to listen to the "best" preachers. The editorial based its opinion on the thinking of Roger W. Babson, statistician and founder of the Babson Statistical Organization.

Babson stated that theological schools should train their graduates to work with the radio instead of competing against it. Graduates should go forth with a sympathetic feeling toward this revolutionary invention and realize its enormous effect and possibilities.

The editorial noted that there will be more churches rather than less churches in the future. However, the smaller churches will use radio preaching to administer to the needs of the congregation regarding exhortations. And the church will have a room that will be kept open day and night with radio preaching so that a person can come at any time and hear the gospel. Babson said, "Personally, I look forward to the day when the Federations of Churches of our different cities can combine and purchase the time for all day Sunday from one of our great national broadcasting chains and thus outbid secular competitors with their jazz contest."

He also pointed out that some people believe that religious broadcasting will increase church attendance, while others think that it causes church attendance to decrease. Babson said that he was not sure which side was right but he believed that there will always be a need for people to have a quiet place in which to worship. It was his opinion that religious broadcasting would increase church attendance and the usefulness of religious services.

Lastly, Babson observed:

"Apparently the churches are in the same situation today that the old guilds were one hundred years ago when the steam engine was invented. The steam engine did not decrease the interest in manufactured goods but rather greatly increased the output of manufactured goods. The method of work was greatly revolutionalized, however, and factories became the means of production and of displacing the guilds. Those who recognized and capitalized on this change were very successful but those who failed to do so fell by the wayside. May not the churches of America be facing a similar situation today? Let us not be like those who fought for hand labor and who refused to adopt looms and spinning machinery."[12]

What's Deregulation?

In additional to numerous other issues, FCC's deregulation considerations also has Christians split. In September 1979, the FCC proposed that the nation's radio stations be deregulated. The proposal called for the elimination of:

Requirements for radio licensees to demonstrate they had addressed the needs and problems of their communities.

Restrictions on the amount of time stations can devote to commercials.

Requirements that a certain amount of time be devoted to non-entertainment programming, such as news and public affairs.

The need for commercial stations to keep detailed logs of their programming for FCC and public inspection.[10]

Paid broadcasters tend to go along with the FCC announcement. They foresee relief from red tape, mounds of paperwork and freedom from hassles with both federal officials and community malcontents.

"Free-timers" are opposed. The church is very much concerned about deregulation, says Michael Bennett, spokesman for the Catholic Church. "Broadcasters should conduct themselves as trustees of the public domain." In a unique unified effort, older mainline churches have asked the FCC to encourage broadcasters to give more free time to religious groups and other charitable organizations. In return, under the terms of the petition before the FCC, the stations would receive credits to recommend them for license renewal.[11]

Walt Cranor, Lutheran Layman's League of the Lutheran Church, Missouri Synod, says that his "Lutheran Hour" would undoubtedly be dropped if stations had no requirement to air programs as a public service. Other free-timers strongly agree with Cranor.[12]

Deregulation, no more clear channel stations, increased research, pay vs no-pay, "holy war" — surely only God could know what the future of this innovative, vivacious and rapidly growing sector of communications —religious radio and television will come to be.

APPENDIX I

(Facsimile of article as it appeared in The Register, January 1942)

RELIGION ON THE AIR IN CHICAGO
A Study of Religious Programs on the Commercial Radio Stations of Chicago
Conducted by Everett C. Parker
Under the direction of Professor Fred Eastman

[To the best of our knowledge this is the first survey of its kind to be published anywhere. Realizing the growing influence of radio in American religious life, the Seminary in 1940 granted Professor Eastman a three months' leave to make exploratory studies in New York in this field. Last spring it assigned to Mr. Everett C. Parker the Curtis Research Fellowship so that the study here reported could be made. Mr. Parker had already had considerable experience as a writer of radio scripts used on a national network and as a director of religious programs on a Chicago station. The authors of the following survey acknowledge gratefully the help of Professor Samuel C. Kincheloe in preparing the questionnaires and in making constructive suggestions.]

Within the last ten years radio has become a powerful force in the life of the people of America. It has affected every phase of that life, and religion is no exception. Religious programs have emerged upon the air without any concerted plan on the part of the great Christian bodies of the nation and today are competing with soap, cigarettes, cosmetics, gasoline, food products, symphony concerts, world news—and even with the churches —for the attention of and, in many instances, for money contributions from the listening public.

This survey of religious radio programs heard in a great metropolitan area was undertaken to determine the extent and nature of such broadcasting and to discover certain facts which might serve as a guide for churches and religious organizations which plan to make use of the radio in the future.

Specific questions were posed regarding religious radio broadcasts in the Chicago area and were embodied in a questionnaire presented to the management of the various commercial radio stations of the Chicago area. Among the facts sought were the following: How much time on the air in a given week is devoted to religious programs? Who sponsors religious broadcasting in Chicago? Who appears on religious programs? What types of programs are presented? Do religious programs make use of all types of radio productions to catch and hold listener interest? Are these programs financed by funds received from appeals made over the air?

To what extent do Chicago listeners receive religious messages over the radio from outside Chicago; that is, do religious programs heard in Chicago originate in other places and reach Chicago through network facilities or transcription? Is the church or the radio studio the point from which most religious broadcasts originate?

The accompanying table lists the 77 religious programs broadcast by Chicago's commercial radio stations with pertinent data concerning each program.

METHOD OF THE SURVEY

The survey was conducted through personal interviews with representatives of the station management. The interviewer visited the stations and filled out the questionnaires in person. Every effot was made to speak with the person who was most familiar both with the policy of the station toward religious broadcasting and with the religious programs of the station. Later, the sponsors of the various programs were asked by mail to answer the same questions put to the stations.

The arbitrary date of the week of November 2 was chosen for the sampling of programs, and only those programs were considered which had been on the air thirteen or more weeks or planned to be broadcast over that minimum period.

All radio stations of the Chicago area were interviewed, and information was obtained from Stations WAAF, WAIT, WBBM, WCFL, WCRW, WEDC, WENR, WGES, WGN, WHFC, WHIP, WIND, WJJD, WLS, WMAQ, WMBI, and WSBC.

Station	Name of Program	Time of Broadcast	Sponsorship	Description
WMAQ 50,000 watts 670 kilocycles N.B.C. Red Network	Radio Pulpit*	Sun., 9:00–9:30 A.M.	Sustaining program† on N.B.C. Red Network under auspices of Federal Council of Churches	Talk by Dr. Ralph Sockman, originating in New York City. Copies of sermons free to listeners. Began: 1932
	National Catholic Hour*	Sun., 5:00–5:30 P.M.	Sustaining program on N.B.C. Red Network under auspices of National Council of Catholic Men	Talk by a Catholic priest, originating in New York City. Various premiums free to listeners. Began: 1930
	Light of the World*	Mon.–Fri., 1:00–1:15 P.M.	Commerical program‡ sponsored by General Mills on N.B.C. Red Network	Dramatizations of the Bible. Began: March, 1940
	Dr. William Stidger	Mon., Wed., Fri., 4:30–4:45 P.M.	Commercial program sponsored locally by *Chicago Daily News*	Talk. Began: July, 1941
	Religion in the News*	Sat., 5:30–5:45 P.M.	Sustaining program on N.B.C. Red Network under auspices of Federal Council of Churches	Religious news commentary by Dr. Walter Van Kirk.
WBBM 50,000 watts 780 kilocycles C.B.S.	Church of the Air*	Sun., 9:00–9:30 A.M.	Sustaining program on C.B.S.	Talks by various ministers of national reputation, originating in various cities. Began: 1933
	Wings over Jordan*	Sun., 9:30–10:00 A.M.	Sustaining program on C.B.S.	Religious songs by "Wings over Jordan" Negro choir. Short talks by Negro ministers. Originates in Cleveland. Began: 1938
	Hymns of All Churches*	Mon., Tue., Thu., 9:00–9:15 A.M.	Commercial program on C.B.S. sponsored by General Mills	Songs by Joe Emerson. Began: 1934
WGN 50,000 watts 720 kilocycles M.B.S. Affiliate	Chicagoland Church Hour	Sun., 9:00–10:00 A.M.	WGN sustaining program	Transcribed broadcast of services of various Chicago area churches of all faiths. Began: October, 1940
	Gospel Singer*	Mon.–Fri., 8:15–8:30 A.M.	Commercial program on M.B.S. (transcribed). Sponsored by Proctor and Gamble	Songs by Edward McHugh
WENR 50,000 watts 890 kilocycles N.B.C. Blue Network	National Vespers*	Sun., 3:00–3:30 P.M.§	Sustaining program on N.B.C. Blue Network under auspices of Federal Council of Churches	A sermon by Dr. Harry Emerson Fosdick and hymns by a quartette, originating in New York City. Copies of sermons free to listeners. Began: 1930

* Indicates a network program.
† Sustaining programs are those for which the station provides broadcast time free of charge.
‡ Commercial programs are those for which the station is paid for the broadcast time used.
§ Not heard in Chicago November 2, 1941, but a regular feature of WENR.

Station	Name of Program	Time of Broadcast	Sponsorship	Description
WENR—*Cont.*	Message of Israel*	Sat., 6:00–6:30 P.M.	Sustaining program on N.B.C. Blue Network under auspices of United Jewish Laymen's Committee	Talks by nationally known rabbis, originating in New York City. Copies of sermons free to listeners. Began: 1934
WLS 50,000 watts 890 kilocycles N.B.C. Blue Network Affiliate	Little Brown Church	Sun., 9:15–10:00 A.M.	WLS sustaining feature	Church service conducted by Dr. John Holland, from studio. Began: 1925
	Old Fashioned Revival Hour*	Sun., 7:00–7:30 P.M.	Sponsored commercially by Gospel Broadcasting Association, Los Angeles, on a special network (transcribed on WLS)	Talk by Rev. Charles E. Fuller. Gospel songs. Contributions solicited
	Morning Devotions	Mon.–Sat., 6:30–6:45 A.M.	WLS sustaining feature	Devotional talks by Dr. John Holland. Began: 1925
	Dinnerbell	Mon.–Sat., 12:25–12:30 P.M.	WLS sustaining feature	Talk by Dr. John Holland. Began: 1925
WJJD 20,000 watts 1160 kilocycles Daytime operation only	Cornell Avenue Church of Christ	Sun., 8:30–9:00 A.M.	Commercial sponsorship by Cornell Avenue Church of Christ	Talk by minister. Began: March, 1940
	Chicago Bible League	Sun., 9:30–9:45 A.M.	Commercial sponsorship by Chicago Bible League	Talk or dramatization
	The People's Church	Sun., 11:00 A.M.–12:30 P.M.	Commercial sponsorship by People's Church (Unitarian)	Church service with Dr. Preston Bradley. Originates in church. Contributions solicited. Began: 1935
	Faith of Our Fathers	Mon.–Sat., 4:30–5:00 A.M.	Commercial sponsorship by Bible Truth Society, Springfield, Mo.	Talk by minister. Funds solicited. Began: September, 1941
	Christian Science	Mon., Wed., Fri., 7:30–7:45 A.M.	Commercial sponsorship by Christian Science Society of Chicago	Talk
	Christian Business Men's Committee	Mon.–Fri., 12:30–1:00 P.M.	Commercial sponsorship by Christian Business Men's Committee	Talks by various ministers. Originates in downtown theater. Funds solicited. Began: 1936
	Family Bible League	Tue.–Sat., 6:30–7:00 A.M.	Commercial sponsorship by Family Bible League	Talk. Bible lessons sold. Began: 1933
	America Back to God	Tue., Thu., Sat., 7:30–7:45 A.M.	Commercial program	Talk. Funds solicited. Began: 1939
WCFL 10,000 watts 1000 kilocycles N.B.C. Affiliate	Southernaires*	Sun., 9:30–10:00 A.M.	Sustaining, N.B.C. Blue Network	Negro quartette singing spirituals. Began: 1937

Station	Name of Program	Time of Broadcast	Sponsorship	Description
WCFL—*Cont.*	Chicago Lutheran Hour	Sun., 2:45–3:00 P.M.	Commercial sponsorship by Aid Association for Lutherans, Appleton, Wis.	Talk. Began: 1939
	National Lutheran Hour*	Sun., 3:00–3:30 P.M.	Commercial sponsorship by Lutheran Laymen's League over special network	Talk by Dr. Walter A. Maier, originating in St. Louis. Funds solicited. Various premiums offered free. Began: 1933
	Young People's Church of the Air*	Sun., 3:30–4:00 P.M.	Commercial sponsorship over special network	Talk by Rev. Percy Crawford, originating in Philadelphia. Funds solicited
	Rosary Hour*	Sun., 4:00–5:00 P.M.	Commercial sponsorship by Rosary Hour Association over special network	Talk by Fr. John Justin, in Polish. Choral music. Originates in Buffalo. Began: 1937
	Back to God	Sun., 6:30–7:00 P.M.	Commercial sponsorship by Christian Reformed Radio Committee	Talk. Funds solicited. Copies of speech free. Began: October, 1941
	Old Fashioned Revival Hour*	Sun., 9:00–10:00 P.M.	*See* WLS	*See* WLS
	Mindfulness of Others	Tue., Thu., Sat., 9:15–9:30 A.M.	Commercial sponsorship by Our Lady of Perpetual Help Catholic Church, Glenview, Ill.	Talks for shut-ins by Fr. John Dussman. Funds solicited. Poems and devotional booklets offered free. Began: 1940
	Novena Hour	Fri., 8:00–9:00 P.M.	Sustaining program under auspices of Our Lady of Sorrows Catholic Church	Novena service. Funds solicited. Began: 1938
	Call to Youth*	Sat., 11:30–11:45 A.M.	Sustaining program on N.B.C. Red Network under auspices of Protestants, Roman Catholics, and Jews	Talks for youth. Began: 1932
WIND (Gary, Ind.) 5,000 watts 560 kilocycles C.B.S. Affiliate	Rumanian Baptist Church of Gary	Sun., 7:30–8:00 A.M.	Commercial sponsorship by Rumanian Baptist Church	Talk in Rumanian. Began: 1935
	Delbert Lighty	Sun., 9:00–9:15 A.M.	Commercial sponsorship by Delbert Lighty	Talk. Began: June, 1941
	Oak Park Pulpit of the Air	Sun., 11:15 A.M.–12:00 M.	Commercial sponsorship by Oak Park First Baptist Church	Church service. Funds solicited. Copies of speech offered free. Began: October, 1940
	Midwest Bible Church	Sun., 5:00–6:00 P.M.	Commercial sponsorship by Midwest Bible Church	Talk. Funds solicited. Began: October, 1941
	First Methodist Church, Gary	Sun., 6:30–7:00 P.M.	Commercial sponsorship by First Methodist Church	Talk. Began: 1933

Station	Name of Program	Time of Broadcast	Sponsorship	Description
WIND—*Cont.*	This Our Mortal Life	Sun., 8:00–8:25 P.M.	Commercial sponsorship by New First Congregational Church	Talk by Dr. O. W. S. McCall. Began: November 2, 1941
	Sunday Evening Club	Sun., 8:30–9:00 P.M.	Sustaining program under auspices of Sunday Evening Club	Talk by religious leaders of national prominence. Originates in Orchestra Hall. Began: 1922
	Old Fashioned Revival Hour*	Sun., 9:00–10:00 P.M.	Commercially sponsored on M.B.S. (*see* WLS)	*See* WLS
	Church of Deliverance	Sun., 11:00–P.M. 12:00 M.	Commercially sponsored by Church of Deliverance (Negro)	Church service. Funds solicited. Began: 1939
WMBI 5,000 watts 1110 kilocycles Daytime operation only	Various religious programs too numerous to mention individually	Sun., 8:00 A.M.–4:30 P.M.; Mon.–Sat., 6:00 A.M.–4:30 P.M.	Station is owned and operated by the Moody Bible Institute. All programs are on a sustaining basis. Included are all types: church services, talks, choruses, dramatizations, news, etc. WMBI is not a commercial station and programs are not included in text summary.	
WHIP (Hammond, Ind.) 5,000 watts 1520 kilocycles Daytime operation only	St. James Methodist Church	Sun., 11:00 A.M.–12:00 M.	Commercially sponsored by St. James Methodist Church	Church service with Dr. Thomas Pender. Funds solicited. Began: November, 1940
	Polish Catholic Messenger	Sun., 2:00–2:30 P.M.	Commercially sponsored	Talk in Polish by Catholic priest
	Rev. George Radeos	Sun., 3:00–3:30 P.M.	Commercially sponsored by First Greek-American Mission	Talk in Greek. Funds solicited. Began: May, 1940
	Ave Maria Hour	Sun., 4:00–4:30 P.M.	Sustaining program under auspices of Graymoor Monastery, Garrison, N.Y. Transcribed	Dramatizations of lives of saints; talk by Catholic monk. Funds solicited. Copies of speech free. Began: 1935
	Roseland Bethany Church Family Altar Service	Sun., 5:00–5:30 P.M.; Mon.–Sat., 7:30–8:00 A.M.	Commercial sponsorship by Roseland Bethany Reformed Church in America	Talk by Rev. Harry Hager, from church. Funds solicited. Began: 1935
	Southtown Church Hour	Mon.–Sat., 12:00 M.–12:15 P.M.	Sustaining program under auspices of Southtown Church–Y.M.C.A. Co-operation Program	Talks by various South Side ministers. Began: 1937
	Christian Science	Tue., 3:00–3:15 P.M.	Commercially sponsored by Christian Science Committee on Publications	Talk. Began: February, 1941

98

Station	Name of Program	Time of Broadcast	Sponsorship	Description
WAIT 1,000 watts 820 kilocycles	Victorious Life Fellowship	Sun., 7:30–8:00 A.M.	Commercial sponsorship by North Side Church of the Nazarene	Talk. Funds solicited. Books given free. Began: December, 1940
	Hebrew-Christian Hour	Sun., 8:00–8:30 A.M.	Commercial sponsorship by First Hebrew-Christian Synagogue, Los Angeles. Transcribed	Talk. Magazine given free. Began: March, 1941
	Lutheran Gospel Hour	Sun., Mon., Wed., Fri., 8:30–9:00 A.M.	Commercial sponsorship by Lutheran Gospel Hour, Elgin, Ill.	Talk. Funds solicited. Plaques given free
	Old Sunday School	Sun., 9:00–10:00 A.M.	Commercial sponsorship by Epiphany Sunday School	Sunday-school lesson from church. Began: 1939
	Moody Memorial Church	Sun., 11:00 A.M.–12:30 P.M.	Commercial sponsorship by Moody Memorial Church	Church service with Rev. H. A. Ironside. Funds solicited. Began: 1934
	Heaven and Home Hour	Sun., 12:30–1:00 P.M.; Mon.–Sat., 7:30–8:00 A.M.	Commercial sponsorship by Chicago Gospel Tabernacle	Talk. Funds solicited. Tracts given free. Began: 1934
	Bible Study Hour	Sun., 1:00–1:30 P.M.; Mon.–Sat., 9:00–9:30 A.M.	Commercial sponsorship by North Shore Church	Church service on Sunday, talks on weekdays, from church. Funds solicited. Began: 1934
	Scripture Truth Hour	Sun., 1:30–2:00 P.M.	Commercial sponsorhip by Scripture Truth Group (laymen)	Bible talk. New Testaments given free. Began: 1938
	Near unto God Hour	Sun., 2:00–2:30 P.M.	Commercial sponsorship by by Rev. John C. Monsma, Grand Rapids, Mich.	Talk. Funds solicited. Began: 1937
	The Life-Line	Mon.–Sat., 8:00–8:15 A.M.	Commercial sponsorship by Northside Gospel Center	Talk. Magazine, songbooks given free. Began: 1939
	Unity Viewpoint	Mon.–Fri., 2:30–2:45 P.M.	Commercial sponsorship by Unity School of Practical Christianity, Kansas City, Mo.	Talk. Began: 1937
	Family Altar	Tue., Thu., Sat., 8:15–8:30 A.M.	Commercial sponsorship by Humboldt Park Gospel Tabernacle	Talk. Funds solicited. Tracts given free. Began: 1938
WAAF 1,000 watts 950 kilocycles Daytime operation only	Metropolitan Church of the Air	Sun., 7:00–7:30 A.M.	Sustaining program of WAAF	Talk by Rev. William Studer. Copies of speech free. Began: 1935

Station	Name of Program	Time of Broadcast	Sponsorship	Description
WGES 1,000 watts (Sundays) 500 watts (weekdays) 1390 kilocycles	Solemn High Mass	Sun., 12:00 M.– 1:00 P.M.	Commercial sponsorship by Our Lady of Sorrows Catholic Church	Mass. Began: 1930
	In Search of Truth	Sun., 6:00– 6:30 P.M.	Commercial sponsorship by Polish Roman Catholic churches of Chicago Archdiocese	Talk in Polish by various priests. Copies of speeches free. Began: 1938
	Gospel Program	Sun., 10:00– 11:00 P.M.	Commercial sponsorship by Humboldt Park Gospel Tabernacle	Church service. Began: September, 1941
WHFC (Cicero) 250 watts (days) 100 watts (nights) 1450 kilocycles	Czech Alliance of Catholics	Sun., 6:30– 7:00 A.M.	Sustaining under auspices of Czech Alliance of Catholics	Talk in Czech by various priest
	Scandinavian Religious Broadcast	Sun., 7:00– 7:45 A.M.	Sustaining under auspices of Cicero Bible Church	Church service in Swedish. Began: 1935
	Cicero Bible Church	Sun., 7:45– 8:30 A.M.; Mon.–Sat., 7:00–7:45 A.M.	Sustaining under auspices of Cicero Bible Church	Church service on Sunday, talk on weekdays. Began: 1935
	First Christian Reformed Church of Cicero	Sun., 3:00– 3:30 P.M.	Sustaining under auspices of First Christian Reformed Church	Talk. Began: 1939
	Evangelical Lutheran Church	Sun., 4:00– 4:30 P.M.	Sustaining under auspices of Redeemer Lutheran Church, Cicero	Talk
	Warren Park Presbyterian Church of Cicero	Sun., 5:30– 6:00 P.M.	Sustaining under auspices of Warren Park Presbyterian Church	Talks in Czech. Dramatizations. Began: 1936
	First Bohemian Baptist Church	Sun., 6:00– 6:30 P.M.	Sustaining under auspices of First Bohemian Baptist Church	Talk in Czech
WSBC 250 watts (days) 100 watts (nights) 1240 kilocycles	Negro Spirituals	Sun., 6:00– 7:00 A.M.	Sustaining program of WSBC	Various Negro choirs singing spirituals. Began: 1936
WEDC 100 watts 1240 kilocycles	Gospel and Spiritual Hour	Sun., 8:30– 9:00 A.M.	Commercial sponsorship by Scotland Credit Clothing Co.	Negro quartette in spirituals. Began: 1935

Station	Name of Program	Time of Broadcast	Sponsorship	Description
WEDC—*Cont.*	Parochial Schools of Chicago	Mon., 4:00–4:15 P.M.	Sustaining program of WEDC	Catholic parochial school choirs. Talk in Czech. Began: 1938
	St. Procopius Catholic Church	Sat., 4:00–4:30 P.M.	Commercial sponsorship by St. Procopius Catholic Church	Talk in Czech by priest. Began: 1935
WCRW 100 watts 1240 kilocycles	NO RELIGIOUS PROGRAMS			

SUMMARY OF FINDINGS

Analysis of the information listed in the table shows that 46 hours of broadcast time each week are devoted to religious programs by Chicago's commercial radio stations. The 77 religious programs heard in these hours constitute 2.9 percent of the total of approximately 1,575 hours that these stations are on the air each week.

most of the religious broadcasting is concentrated on Sunday, 54 of the 77 programs being on the air that day. Of the total number of programs, 56 are heard only once a week, while only 14 are on the air as often as five times a week. Programs tend to be of one of two types: an actual church service (13 programs) or predominantly a sermon or talk (57 programs). For the most part religious broadcasting is concentrated in large doses; 43 of the 77 programs studied are one-half hour in length, 12 are on the air a full hour and 2 run one and a half hours.

Denominational and Doctrinal Character

Of the 77 religious programs, 14 are interdenominational in scope, 41 are Protestant, 11 are Roman Catholic, 1 is Jewish, 2 are Christian Science and 8 have no denominational affiliation.

The majority of the 41 Protestant programs are fundamentalist in

101

character, 25 programs, or 61 percent of the total, being sponsored by local churches or religious organizations which profess fundamentalist doctrines. (Note that these figures do not include the programs broadcast over WMBI, all of which are fundamentalist in nature.) Only 3 of the remaining Protestant programs may be classed as liberal in character, the rest being of orthodox and conservative nature.

The 14 interdenominational programs are of varying classification with respect to doctrine. One is fundamentalist (see Station WAAF); one is mixed, welcoming all shades of opinion ("Southtown Church Hour," Station WHIP); and one is a choral program and cannot be classified on a doctrinal basis ("Negro Spirituals," Station WSBC). The remaining 11 interdenominational programs profess and maintain a liberal viewpoint.

Who Pays the Bills?

To a large extent Religion on the Air in Chicago pays for itself. Of the 77 programs, 49 are commercial; and, of these, 22 are sponsored by local churches. However, it should be noted that many of the programs which would cost the most for broadcast time are sustaining features rather than commercial. These latter include the nin sustaining programs on the NBC and CBS networks, the "Chicagoland Church Hour" on WGN, and the sustaining programs on WLS.

A noteworthy feature of Protestant religious programs in Chicago is that, while nine denominations of national scope are represented on the air, no program receives support from denominational funds. As far as could be ascertained, only two programs—St. James Methodist Church on WHIP and the Christian Reformed Church's "Back to God" on WCFL—are presented with the endorsement of their respective denominations.

The Audience

It is difficult to determine the influence on the radio audience of the religious programs heard in Chicago, and it is impossible to estimate the size of this audience with any degree of accuracy. Certain factors which tend to show that the audience is sizable are: (1) 49 programs are sponsored commercially and 18 originate in churches or other remote points, requiring the rental of telephone lines; (2) two of the largest national radio advertisers have found that network religious programs will sell their products; (3) 33 programs depend upon contributions from listeners for at least a part of their support; and (4) network religious programs and several local religious programs have a substantial mail response. That the audience of religious programs is loyal in its listening habits is apparent from the fact that 29 programs have been on the air from one to five years, while 30 others have been broadcasting more than five years.

Station Policy

In general, the management of the commercial radio stations in the Chicago area agrees that religious programs fall into the category of public service features and that all denominations and sects are entitled to representation on the air. However, the major stations (i.e., those with 50,000 watts power and a clear channel—WMAQ, WBBM, WGN, WENR, WLS) and Station WAAF go even further and refuse to accept religious programs for boradcasting on a commercial basis.

The attitude of these stations is typified by the statement of policy published by the National Broadcasting Company on January 9, 1939: "The National Broadcasting Company does not sell time for religious programs as this course might result in according a disproportionate representation to those individuals or groups who chance to command the largest purses."

The National Broadcasting Company serves only the central or national agencies of great religious faiths as distinguished from individual churches or group movements where national membership is comparatively small. In effect this policy limits religious programs hear in Chicago over the NBC networks to those presented under the auspices of the National Council of Catholic Men, the Federal Council of Churches of Christ in America, and the United Jewish Laymen's Committee.

The Columbia Broadcasting System follows substantially the same policy as NBC but creates its religious programs without the cooperation of national religious agencies. The Mutual Broadcasting System sells its facilities to religious organizations, but WGN, its Chicago affiliate, will not carry commercial religious programs.

Other stations in Chicago are willing to sell broadcast time to religious organizations and local churches, and it is through their facilities that religious programs may be broadcast on a commercial basis.

WMBI is licensed as an educational station which may not accept commercial programs. The station is owned and operated by the Moody Bible Institute, which produces most of its programs. However, the facilities of the station are open on a sustaining basis to religious roganizations which conform to the policy and doctrines of the Institute. WMBI broadcasts approximately 100 different programs each week, all of a religious nature. The station has pioneered in adapting successful commercial broad-casting techniques to religious programs and lists among its features round tables, religious news commentaries, quiz programs, dramatizations and pro-grams of fine music. All of these techniques are devoted to advancing the fundamentalist doctrines of the Institute.

CONCLUSIONS

Up to this point the findings of the survey have been presented factually and objectively. But the reader may naturally ask: "What conclu-sions do you who have made this study draw from these findings?" Here we are in the realm of interpretation and opinion, but the question is a fair one and deserves an answer. Here are four conclusions:

1. The religious programs on the air seem overloaded with talk. Note again the fact that fifty-seven of them are predominantly devoted to sermons or addresses and thirteen to actual church services, including a sermon.

2. Many of the religious programs are of a low quality artistically and their religious value is doubtful. They lack dignity. Many of the minis-ters seem to play upon the credulity, the sentimentality, the superstitions and the fears of their audiences. Their appeals for money are often blatant but apparently they are sufficiently effective to bring in enough money to pay the costs of the broadcasts and perhaps even to make them profitable.

3. The network programs of the National Broadcasting Company and the Columbia Broadcasting System are of a much higher order. Especi-ally acceptable to Protestant audiences are NBC's "National Vesters" (Harry Emerson Fosdick preaching) and "The Radio Pulpit" (Ralph Sockman preaching) and C.B.S.'s "Wings over Jordan" and "The Church of the Air." Yet two factors concerning these network programs should be borne in mind: (a) They are by no means available over all the stations on the networks. Throughout the autumn of 1941, for example, no N.B.C. station in the Chicago area carried Dr. Fosdick—he was crowded off the air in favor of professional Sunday football. (b) They are expensive programs to main-tain. Even though the networks donate the time, from $250 to $350 must be raised for each thirty-minute broadcast to pay the necessary costs for musicians and for mimeographing and postage for mailing out the sermons to those who request them.

4. Too many of the network programs, expecially those of

N.B.C., originate from New York. While this has a certain advantage in keeping other parts of the country in touch with the thought and feeling of New York ministers, it might be well for the New York area and the Atlantic seaboard to hear the thoughts and feelings of ministers in other sections of the country.

RECOMMENDATIONS

The reader may also ask, "What is to be done to improve the quality of religious programs on the air?" With more diffidence than may seem apparent, the following recommendations are offered for the consideration of churches and religious broadcasters:

1.   Less talk and more great religious music would be welcome. The greatest composers in the world have devoted their talents to the writing of religious music, yet there is not a single radio program devoted to the presentation of the masterpieces in this field. It is worth remembering that during the last world's fair in Chicago, the churches presented religion through the Temple of Religion, where the programs and exhibits were largely devoted to talks and propaganda for various church agencies. The Time and Fortune Building, on the other hand, provided quiet rooms for rest and reading with occasional music, where weary people could relax and meditate. Thousands of visitors found the Time and Fortune Building of more religious value to them than the Temple of Religion.

2.   The churches should study how to create types of programs that fit the peculiar facilities of radio. The "Town Meeting of the Air," the "Music Appreciation Hour," and the "American School of the Air" have developed such techniques in the field of secular education. Why should they not be used in religious education?

The "Calvacade of America" has successfully dramatized American history. A similar technique applied to the history of the great religious movements and personalities of the ages might be equally or even more effective. Only three of the programs now employ dramatization to present their religious message, yet one of these — "The Light of the World," dramatizing stories based upon the Bible — has one of the largest audiences of any religious type program. (It is commercially sponsored by General Mills, Inc.)

Round-table discussions, forums, and even the much-abused quiz technique which, though difficult, have all proved their worth on the air, are entirely ignored by religious agencies. Equally ignored is the technique of the

"Ford Sunday Evening Hour," where a brief five-minute talk is inserted in the middle of a fine musical program.

All radio broadcasting is expensive, and programs of the type just suggested will be beyond the possibilities of the local church. Their production will call for concerted planning on the part of national denominations and interdenominational agencies.

APPENDIX II

(Facsimile of article as it appeared in Journal of Broadcasting, Vol. XVI, No. 1 (Winter 1971-72)

WHO LISTENS TO RELIGIOUS RADIO BROADCASTS ANYMORE?
by
Ronald L. Johnstone

During his 1966-69 tenure as director of research for the Lutheran Council in the U.S.A., Ronald L. Johnstone helped plan and conduct the research reported here which is based on a sizable national sample. In the article, he constructs a profile of the typical religious radio program listener. Dr. Johnstone earned the Ph.D. from the University of Michigan in 1963 and is now associate professor of sociology at Central Michigan University in Mt. Pleasant.

Although hundreds of local radio stations throughout the country program religious broadcasts and although countless religious groups sponsor and encourage such programs, very little is known about how many people listen, or above all who they are. Some current data to answer these questions are now available—data that were gathered by the author and the National Opinion Research Center as an integral part of a national survey conducted in 1970 by the Lutheran Council in the U.S.A. concerning the "image of Lutheranism."

One goal of this project was to answer the above questions for Lutheran radio and television programs. But a control question was also asked about religious radio programs generally. Our initial and major concern will be at this general or total level: Who, how often, how many? In the second part of the paper we'll look at a specific case in point—the *Lutheran Hour* radio program.

The Religious Radio Audience

First, how many people listen and how frequently do they listen to religious radio programs of any type? The data in Table I show a nearly even split between those who listen at least occasionally and those who essentially never do. The data in Table I are of interest as they stand, probably of considerable interest particularly to those who may have thought nobody listened to religious radio programs anymore. To find that nearly half of the United States adult population listens to a religious radio program at least occasionally seems to be a significant finding and in absolute terms the proportion of 48% seems fairly high. It should be noted that these data are strikingly similar to those in Casmir's 1957 study. He found in Los Angeles that 24% of the respondents listened "regularly" (cf. 20% "Often" in our sample). Although Casmir's data are from only one metropolitan area and used telephone interviews while our sample is national and utilized a personal interview, the similarities in the data are fascinating, particularly because one could be led to suggest that no great change in proportions of persons listening to religious radio programs has taken place since 1957.

TABLE I

Frequency of Listening to Religious Radio Programs
(Proportion and Number of U. S. Adult Population)

Frequency	Number	Proportion
Often	303	20%
Occasionally	418	28
Seldom	393	26
Never	376	25
Not Ascertained	4	0
TOTALS	1490	99%

Informative as the summary data may be, however, it will be more instructive to identify the listeners. Who are these people who listen to religious radio broadcasts? In answer to this question we intend to look for significant differences among the listeners and the non-listeners along several important control dimensions such as denominational affiliation, age, sex, educational level, geographic region, degree of religious commitment and interest, frequency of attendance at religious services, and urban/rural residence.

TABLE II

FREQUENCY OF LISTENING TO RELIGIOUS RADIO PROGRAMS
BY VARIOUS CHARACTERISTICS OF RESPONDENTS

	Often	Occasionally	Seldom	Never	NA	Total N
A. RELIGIOUS OR DENOMINATIONAL PREFERENCE*						
Protestant	26%	31%	25%	18%		976
Baptist	37	31	20	13		333
Episcopal	13	22	28	38		32
Lutheran	13	34	32	22		120
Methodist	18	34	33	15		187
Presbyterian	19	30	19	31	1	67
United Church of Christ	24	29	26	22		51
Other Protestant	30	26	27	17	1	156
Catholic	8	25	30	37		355
Jew	13	17	25	46		24
Other	26	17	24	33		42
None	11	18	27	45		93
B. FREQUENCY OF CHURCH ATTENDANCE*						
Every or nearly every Sunday	23%	31%	27%	19%		652
Once or twice a month	25	30	26	18		273
A few times a year	16	28	27	30		222
Hardly ever	16	21	26	37	1	172
Never	11	21	24	44		74
Don't Know	100					1
C. IMPORTANCE OF RELIGION*						
Very important	27%	31%	24%	18%		978
Somewhat important	8	25	33	34		306
Not very or not at all important	3	17	30	49	2	112
D. AGE*						
18-29	11%	16%	31%	42%		329
30-39	17	22	31	30		246
40-49	22	30	25	23	1	274
50-59	23	36	22	19		235
60-69	27	30	28	16		217
70 and older	27	43	18	42		181
E. SEX						
Male	20%	27%	30%	23%	1	640
Female	21	29	24	27		850
F. EDUCATION*						
Less than eight	32%	30%	21%	18%		370
9-11	25	29	24	22		306
High school graduate	15	28	30	27		468
Some college	11	28	30	30	1	208
College graduate	7	30	29	34		98
Graduate school	21	10	33	37		52
G. GEOGRAPHIC REGION OF RESIDENCE*						
Northeast	13%	28%	24%	35%		357
Midwest	18	29	29	23		419
Southeast	30	38	21	16		213
South	34	28	24	14		258
Mountain and Pacific	13	23	31	33	1	243
H. URBAN/RURAL RESIDENCE*						
Large metropolitan	15%	22%	24%	39%	1	330
Small metropolitan	21	28	26	25		615
Non-metropolitan town	20	35	28	16		233
Rural	26	30	28	16		312

*All parts of Table II marked with an asterisk are statistically significant at the .01 level using chi square.

Denominational Affiliations: From Table II-A it is most clear that Protestants generally are far more likely than any other category to listen to religious radio broadcasts. This finding is again consistent with the Casmir data (67% Protestant and 42% Catholic regular and occasional listeners compared with 57% Protestant and 33% Catholic frequent and occasional listeners in our sample). As would be expected, Jews and those professing no religious identification are least likely to listen. What is probably most surprising at first glance is that Catholics barely outdistance those respondents of Jewish or no affiliation in the frequency with which they listen. This discovery is probably essentially explained by the preponderance of Protestant radio programs across the country.

But what about the various denominations within Protestantism? The data in Table II-A show that the differences among those who listen often or at least occasionally are not great. Only the Baptists truly distinguish themselves as being most likely to listen. If we look only at those who listen often we find included a fairly high proportion of the "other Protestant" category. This category includes the smaller Protestant groups, particularly those of a fundamentalistic and sectarian character. Episcopalians and Presbyterians cluster near the other end of the continuum with 38% and 31% respectively reporting they never listen to religious radio broadcasts.

Frequency of Attendance at Religious Services: Theoretically one might expect a difference here. That is, the more frequent attenders will be more likely to listen to religious radio because they are presumably more "religious" or at least more likely to support what the religious institutions sponsor. The data in Table II-B support the prediction: there is a positive relationship between frequency of church attendance and frequency of listening to religious radio programs. This supports earlier findings of Casmir and of Parker, Barry, and Smythe in which those who are in church Sunday mornings are more likely to hear a religious message on radio than the absent ones.

Importance of Religion: As is seen in Table II-C, there is a positive relationship between respondents' judgments about the importance of religion in their lives and the frequency with which they listen to religious radio broadcasts. Again we see the reinforcement function of radio religion for those who are already in touch with religious institutions, but there is relatively little contact with the uninitiated and the minimally committed.

Age of Respondents: Table II-D shows a highly significant positive

110

relationship between age and frequency of listening to religious radio programs. In fact if we combine the "often" with the "occasional" listeners we find a range of 28% of the youngest respondents (18-29 years of age) to 70% of the oldest respondents (70 years plus). Certainly there are many reasons for this dramatic range of proportions. One immediately thinks of such factors as less extra-domicile activities on the part of older persons, older persons having established radio listening patterns in the pre-television years, older persons having greater interest in traditional religious forms and presentations which religious radio broadcasts tend to repeat. Despite likely relevance of these and other factors, however, the relationship between age and likelihood or frequency of listening to religious radio still stands as significant.

Sex of Respondents: Table II-E, however, shows no difference in the frequency of listening to religious radio programs between males and females. The traditional observation that women are more religious than men does not carry over to differential listening to religious radio broadcasts.

Education: We would expect less listening to religious radio broadcasts with increasing education. The data in Table II-F support this expectation. There is a steady increase in the proportion of respondents who never listen as education increases. The only anomaly in the entire table is the 21% of the highest educational category who report that they often listen to religious programs on the radio. This discrepancy essentially disappears, however, when we combine the categories of "often" and "occasionally." The proportions are then a direct regression from the lowest to the highest educational category (62%, 54%, 43%, 39%, 37%, 31%).

Geographic Region: It could reasonably be hypothesized that since the midwest and south are Protestant strongholds, and with the heavy Baptist concentration in the south particularly, that these two regions would exceed the others in frequency of listening to religious radio programs. Table II-G reveals clear support for this expectation. Residents of the southern states, followed by those in the midwest, significantly exceed residents in the northeastern, Pacific, and mountain states in frequency of listening to religious radio broadcasts. In reality, as already suggested, differential denominational concentration seems to spell the difference.

Urban/Rural Differences: The data in Table II-H again show significant differences. In this case the farther removed from urban centers the more likely to listen to religious radio. The progression is continuous if the two categories of "often" and "occasional" listening are combined.

We have just run through a number of factors that significantly affect the frequency of listening to religious radio broadcasts. Putting them together into some sort of composite portrait of the frequent or at least occasional listener to religious broadcasts we find the following: an older person of either sex, likely to live in a southern state and in a small town or rural area, of relatively little education, of Protestant religious commitment, a Baptist Protestant in particular, who attends his church for religious services nearly every Sunday, and regards religion as an important feature in his life. Stated another way, religious radio broadcasts appear to be quite unlikely to reach the non-Christian or minimally committed or involved Christian, the young, the highly educated and those of urban residence.

A Specific Example

Without going into undue detail it is instructive to look more specifically at a case in point; i.e., one of the oldest continuous religious radio programs with a worldwide audience—the *Lutheran Hour*. Although no one could pretend to assume that this program is representative of all religious radio programs, it has been on the air for 40 years and has been at one time or another available on nearly every radio dial in the nation. If any religious radio program has had length and breadth of potential exposure, this one has. In 1943 *Time* reported 12 million listeners, or approximately 9% of the United States population. How does this broadcast rate today against this benchmark, vague and unsubstantiated though it is, and against the data reported earlier in this paper?

By way of answer to this question we asked respondents: "Have you ever heard of the *Lutheran Hour* radio program?" and followed with probes as appropriate into whether they ever listened to it and how often. We found that despite its longevity more than half the U. S. population have never heard of this program (52%), let alone listened to it. On the other hand, 27% of the population do listen to it at least occasionally. Actually the latter proportion is probably a more striking one than the former inasmuch as this is a denominational program, though one that naturally tries to reach beyond its own circle. In fact, although disproportionate to their numbers in the population, Lutherans constitute only 14% of those who have heard of the *Lutheran Hour* radio program and 19% of those who have at some time listened to it. Obviously it has reach beyond the Lutheran denomination. But does its reach differ from that of religious programs generally? We are thinking here of the limitations discovered in the first part of this paper with respect to the audience for religious radio broadcasts. We'll proceed with the control variables used before.

Table III reveals some dramatic differences in awareness and contact with this denominational radio program by the denominational preference of respondents. Protestants, Lutherans in particular, are more likely to have heard of and listened to the *Lutheran Hour* than Catholics, Jews, and other non-Christians, and those with no affiliation. Here again we have obvious additional support for the earlier observation that religious radio programs are significantly most likely to be tuned in by those persons already closest to what the program stands for and has to say.

TABLE III

Familiarity with the LUTHERAN HOUR by Denominational Preference

Denomination	Heard of it		Listened to it	
	N	%	N	%
Catholic	136	38	65	18
Baptist	134	40	77	23
Episcopalian	18	56	11	34
Lutheran	96	80	75	63
Methodist	108	58	58	31
Presbyterian	46	69	20	30
United Church of Christ	26	51	15	29
Other Protestant	83	53	47	30
Protestant (unspecified)	10	39	2	8
Jewish	5	21	2	8
Other non-Christian	14	33	7	17
No religious preference	33	35	18	19

Paralleling our former data we observe that frequency of listening to the *Lutheran Hour* is positively related to frequency of church attendance. That is, the proportion of those who ever listen to the *Lutheran Hour* ranges from 23% of the frequent church attendees to 8% of those who hardly ever or never attend church.

A nearly identical pattern emerges when we look at the "importance of religion" variable. The proportion of those who never have listened to the *Lutheran Hour* ranges from 69% of those who consider religion "very important" to them personally through 79% of those who see it as "somewhat important" to 89% of those who report religion as "not very" or "not at all" important in their lives.

Most of the demographic variables we looked at before for religious radio programs generally show a similar pattern when used as control variables affecting the listening to our example of a specific religious radio broadcast. A summary of the impact of these variables on the frequency of listening to the *Lutheran Hour* follows:

(a) *Age:* The proportion of those who ever listen to the *Lutheran Hour* ranges from 15% of the youngest age category to 37% of the oldest.

(b) *Sex:* As with the general question about religious radio programs, there are no differences between males and females in the frequency of listening to the particular example of the *Lutheran Hour* (72% of men and 75% of women never listen).

(c) *Education:* Although we found earlier an inverse relationship between amount of formal education and frequency of listening to religious radio broadcasts, this difference does not hold for the *Lutheran Hour*. Not that the relationship is reversed. There simply is no significant difference related to formal education. For example, 18% of those with less than a high school education compare with 20% of college graduates who listen to the *Lutheran Hour* at least occasionally.

(d) *Geographic Region:* Listeners to the *Lutheran Hour* are clearly concentrated in the midwest which is more than coincidentally the stronghold of Lutheranism. But there is no significantly high listenership in the south as had been the case for religious radio programs generally. What we have here is further evidence that denominational preference makes a difference in the listening patterns of people so far as religious radio programs are concerned and that people do not listen to them indiscriminately. That is, Southerners, though more likely than others to listen to religious radio broadcasts are not more likely than others to listen to the *Lutheran Hour* even though the *Lutheran Hour* is broadcast throughout the South. Southerners are probably listening to their own denominational

114

programs.

(e)   *Urban/Rural Residence:* Listeners to the *Lutheran Hour* are clearly more likely to be residents of non-metropolitan towns and rural areas (as we found earlier to be true of listeners to religious programs generally). In fact, there is a direct decrease in those who have never listened to the program as one moves from large metropolitan communities. The proportions of those who never listen are 84% in large metropolitan centers, 76% in small metropolitan communities, and 63% in non-metropolitan and rural areas.

In looking at our particular example of a religious radio program, we have found no surprises but lots of support for our earlier discoveries. In essence they are epitomized in our earlier statement to the effect that religious radio programs serve primarily a reinforcement function. This observation has found additional solid support from the data concerning the *Lutheran Hour*. Lutherans are far more likely than anyone else to listen to it.

Summary

In brief, religious radio broadcasting tends to reach those who have already been reached in the sense of already having formal association with religious institutions. The old, the church member, the regular attender—these comprise the large majority of the listening audience for religious radio broadcasts.

Who listens to religious radio anymore? Does anyone? Certainly. Many do. But it seems very clear from the foregoing data that the question of who is more important and revealing than the more frequent question of how many. That is, neither high nor low numbers reveal whether those listening are being reached by other religious institutional means. Our data indicate that most of the listeners are already fairly firmly attached to institutional religion.

Facsimile of Unpublished Doctoral Dissertation

RELIGIOUS BROADCASTING IN SOUTHERN CALIFORNIA
By George Hill

This survey was conducted to determine the attitudes of people in Long Beach and Los Angeles concerning religious radio and television, especially since there are 13 religious radio and two religious television stations in Southern California. The goal of the project was to determine who viewed/ listened, when, was money contributed, apparent sincerity of broadcasters, are people being saved by viewing/listening.

The total sample studies was 372 people, relative to religious broadcasting. Of the 372 respondents, 208 were from the greater Los Angeles area (Group A) and 164 were from the Long Beach area (Group B).

Tables 1-5 present the Descriptive Analysis of the sample group.

TABLE 1
RACE

Race	Group A		Group B	
Black	(29)	17%	(37)	38%
Latin	(03)	3%	(15)	15%
Asian	(10)	10%	(01)	1%
White	(63)	69%	(45)	46%

As can be observed from Table 1, most of the respondents were under the classification of White in both groups A and B. The race with the second highest number of respondents was Black in both groups A and B. The race with the least representation of respondents was Latin in Group A and Asian in Group B.

TABLE 2

AGE

Age	Group A		Group B	
25-35 years	(11)	10%	(14)	14%
36-45 years	(28)	27%	(51)	52%
46-55 years	(60)	57%	(09)	9%
56 and over	(06)	6%	(24)	24%
	(105)	100%	(98)	99%

Table 2 shows that respondents between the ages of 46 and 55 in Group A had the highest representation and respondents between the ages of 36 and 45 in Group B had the highest representation. It can also be observed that the least number of respondents in Group A was in the group 56 and over and the least number of respondents in Group B was in the group 46 to 55 years.

It can be observed from Table 3 that most of the respondents had at least a high school education. The least number of respondents in both Group A and Group B attended graduate school. It can also be observed that a greater number of respondents in Group B had only an elementary education than in Group A.

117

TABLE 3
EDUCATION

Education	Group A		Group B	
Elementary	(08)	8%	(29)	30%
High School	(61)	58%	(42)	43%
Undergraduate School	(27)	25%	(22)	22%
Graduate School	(09)	9%	(05)	5%
	(105)	100%	(98)	100%

TABLE 4
INCOME

Income	Group A		Group B	
Above $15,000	(58)	55%	(48)	49%
Below $15,000	(47)	45%	(50)	51%
	(105)	100%	(98)	100%

Table 4 shows that the majority of the respondents income in Group A was above $15,000 a year and in Group B the majority of the respondents income was below $15,000 a year.

TABLE 5
SEX

Sex	Group A		Group B	
Male	(51)	48%	(40)	41%
Female	(54)	51%	(58)	59%

Table 5 shows that the majority of the respondents in Group A were females and the majority of the respondents in Group B were males.

TABLE 6
RESPONSES TO THE QUESTION: DO YOU WATCH TV OR LISTEN TO THE RADIO?

	Response		
	Yes		No
Group A	(208)	56%	0
Group B	(164)	44%	0
	372	100%	0

Table 6 shows that out of 208 people surveyed in the Los Angeles area, all 208 people watched TV or listened to the radio. Table 6 also shows that out of 164 people surveyed in the Long Beach area, all 164 people watched TV or listened to the radio.

TABLE 7
RESPONSES TO THE QUESTION: DO YOU WATCH OR LISTEN TO ANY RELIGIOUS BROADCASTS?

| | Response | |
	Yes	No
Group A	105	103
Group B	98	66

Table 7 shows that out of 208 people in the Los Angeles area, 105 watched or listened to religious broadcasts while 103 did not. Table 7 also shows that out of 164 people in the Long Beach area only 98 people watched or listened to religious broadcasts while 66 did not.

TABLE 8
RESPONSES TO THE QUESTION: DO YOU WATCH RELIGIOUS PROGRAMS ON TV?

| | Responses | | | | |
	Yes	No	0	SO	SE
Group A	(93) 89%	(11) 10%	41	20	33
Group B	(80) 82%	(18) 18%	36	18	18

Table 8 shows that out of the five responses given, the majority of the respondents answered yes to the question in Group A and in Group B. The respondents could have answered either: yes, no, often (0), Sometimes (SO), or Seldom (SE). Of the 208 people in Group A the least number of people answered "no" and out of the 164 people in Group B, the least number of people answered "no" and "seldom".

TABLE 9
RESPONSES TO THE QUESTION: DO YOU LISTEN TO RELIGIOUS PROGRAMS ON RADIO?

	Responses				
	Yes	No	0	SO	SE
Group A	(45) 43%	(60) 57%	25	9	33
Group B	(45) 46%	(53) 50%	26	28	15

It can be observed from Table 9 that the majority of the respondents in both Group A and Group B responded "no" to the question. In Group A the least amount of people responded "SO" (sometimes) and in Group B, the least amount of people responded "SE" (seldom).

TABLE 10
RESPONSES TO THE QUESTION: DO YOU EVER CONTRIBUTE MONEY?

	Responses				
	Yes	No	0	SO	SE
Group A	(28) 21%	(77) 58%	9	5	14
Group B	(31) 24%	(67) 52%	15	10	6

$$x^2 = 1.9732, p \quad .05$$

By examining the data presented in Table 10, it may be seen that there was not a signficant difference in the frequency which Group A and Group B contributed money to religious broadcasting programs. This fact is substantiated by the computed value of the chi square at 1.9734 which indicates that there is not a signficant difference between the two groups at the .05 level.

TABLE 11

RESPONSES TO THE QUESTION: HAVE YOU EVER ATTENDED ANY
MEETINGS THAT WERE MADE KNOWN TO YOU BY A RELIGIOUS
BROADCAST?

	Responses			
	Yes		No	
Group A	(18)	19%	(87)	88%
Group B	(21)	21%	(77)	78%

$$x^2 = 1.4312, p \quad .05$$

By observing the data presented in Table 11, it may be noted that
there was not a significant difference in the frequency which Group A and
Group B attended meetings that were made known by religious broadcasting.
This fact is substantiated by the computed value of the chi square at 1.4312
which indicates that there is not a significant difference between the two
groups at the .05 level.

TABLE 12

RESPONSES TO THE QUESTION: DO YOU WATCH OR LISTEN TO
RELIGIOUS BROADCASTING ON SUNDAY?

	Responses			
	Yes		No	
Group A	(95)	90%	(10)	10%
Group B	(90)	92%	(08)	8%

$$x^2 = 0.7513, p \quad .05$$

By examining the data presented in Table 12, it may be seen that
there was not a significant difference in the frequency in which Group A and
Group B watched or listened to religious broadcasting on Sundays. This fact
is substantiated by the computed value of the chi square at 0.7513 which

indicates that there is not a significant difference between the two groups at the .05 level.

TABLE 13

RESPONSES TO THE QUESTION: DO YOU WATCH OR LISTEN TO RELIGIOUS BROADCASTING ON WEEKDAYS?

| | Responses | | | |
	Yes		No	
Group A	(24)	23%	(81)	77%
Group B	(32)	33%	(66)	67%

$$x^2 = 0.6143, p \quad .05$$

By examining the data presented in Table 13, it may be noted that there was not a significant difference in the frequency in which Group A and Group B watched or listened to religious broadcasting on weekdays. This fact is substantiated by the computed value of the chi square at 0.6143 which indicates that there is not a significant difference between the two groups at the .05 level.

TABLE 14

RESPONSES TO THE QUESTION: HAS LISTENING OR VIEWING THE BROADCAST CAUSED YOU OR ANYONE ELSE YOU KNOW TO BE SAVED?

| | Responses | | | |
	Yes		No	
Group A	(16)	15%	(89)	85%
Group B	(09)	9%	(89)	91%

$$x^2 = 2.3141, p \quad .05$$

123

By examining the data presented in Table 14, it may be noted that there was not a signficant difference in the frequency which Group A and Group B was saved or anyone else that they knew was saved by listening to the broadcast. This fact is substantiated by the computed value of the chi square at 2.3141 which indicates that there is not a significant difference between the two groups at the .05 level.

TABLE 15

RESPONSES TO THE QUESTION: HAS VIEWING OR LISTENING AIDED YOU OR ANYONE YOU KNOW IN GIVING UP A BAD HABIT?

	Responses			
	Yes		No	
Group A	(21)	20%	(84)	80%
Group B	(15)	15%	(83)	83%

$$x^2 = 3.4214, p \quad .05$$

By examining the data presented in Table 15, it may be seen that there was not a signficant difference in the frequency in which Group A and Group B gave up or anyone they knew gave up any bad habits by viewing or listening to religious broadcasting. This fact is substantiated by the computed value of the chi square at 3.4214 which indicates that there is not a significant difference between the two groups at the .05 level.

TABLE 16

RESPONSES TO QUESTION: ARE YOU A MEMBER OF A CHURCH TEMPLE, ETC.?

	Responses			
	Yes		No	
Group A	(44)	42%	(61)	58%
Group B	(37)	37%	(61)	61%

$$x^2 = 2.1473, p \quad .05$$

By observing the data in Table 16, it can be seen that there was not a significant difference in the frequency in which Group A and Group B was a member of a church, temple, etc. This fact was substantiated by the computed value of the chi square at 2.1473 which indicates that there is not a significant difference between the two groups at the .05 level.

TABLE 17

RESPONSES TO THE QUESTION: DO YOU FEEL THAT PEOPLE
ENGAGED IN RELIGIOUS BROADCASTING ARE SINCERE
AND DEEPLY RELIGIOUS?

	Responses			
	Yes		No	
Group A	(54)	51%	(51)	49%
Group B	(48)	49%	(50)	51%

$$x^2 = 3.0141, p \quad .05$$

By examining the data presented in Table 17, it may be noted that there was not a significant difference in the frequency in which Group A and Group B felt that people engaged in religious broadcasting were sincere and deeply religious. This fact is substantiated by the computed value of the chi square at 3.0141 which indicated that there is not a significant difference between the two groups at the .05 level.

TABLE 18

RESPONSES TO THE QUESTION: IS THERE A NEED FOR A
RELIGIOUS REVIVAL IN OUR SOCIETY TODAY?

	Responses			
	Yes		No	
Group A	(21)	22%	(74)	78%
Group B	(33)	34%	(65)	66%

$$x^2 = 3.970, p \quad .05$$

The replies by the respondents to this question were significantly different. A much larger portion of the subjects from Group B felt that there is a need for a religious revival in our society today. This is corroborated by the fact that the chi square reached a significant level (.05) of difference.

Summary and Conclusions

The purpose of the study has been to examine the various aspects of religious broadcasting and to determine what influence, if any, that it has had on the listening public. It was noted that there is an intense competition between the various factions of broadcasting to influence the thinking of man. Mass communication bases its values on commodity which are keyed to the needs of the mass production industries of the mass consumption markets.

In such a situation the church, in its broadcasting, must maintain ideals which are characteristic of a wholesome society and it must profess faith and hope for humanity. This is true due to the fact that Christian objectives are as relevant as they ever were. The need for spiritual health is as important a need, as profound a longing, and as redemptive for twentieth-century Americans as was in the first century for Romans, Jews, and Greeks.

The study examined the history of religious broadcasting in America beginning in the 1920's. It was found that the sermon was the format for a religious program in the beginning. This format was retained until the 1960's, generally speaking. It was in the 1960's that new efforts at innovative format became prominent in religious broadcasting. But, most of these approaches were limited to television.

It was found that when free time is provided for religious broadcasting — it is not during prime time. This is true because the religious broadcast would be competing with wealthy commercial institutions for prime audience time, and religious groups have often found it difficult paying for prime time. When religious broadcasting becomes a funding problem, program production is somewhat inferior. Peter Elderveld, Fulton Sheen, M. R. De Haan, Charles E. Couglin, and Aimee Semple McPherson used most of their funds for buying air time. This left little money for program production.

The contributions of Bishop Sheen, The Lutheran Hour, Bob Shuler, Aimee Semple McPherson, Rex Humbard, Oral Roberts and Billy Graham were also examined. A survey was made to compare the influence on people who live in Long Beach and Los Angeles of religious broadcasting.

The Conclusions

Based on the findings in Chapter IV, the following conclusions are presented.

1. Group A and Group B did not differ significantly regarding matching religious programs on TV.
2. The two groups did not have a signficant difference relative to listening to religious broadcasting.
3. There was not a signficant difference between Group A and Group B on the amount of money which they contribute to religious broadcasting.
4. Most of the subjects from the City of Long Beach and from the City of Los Angeles did not contribute to religious broadcasting.
5. There was not a significant difference in the attendance of residents of Long Beach and residents of Los Angeles relative to attending religious affairs sponsored by religious broadcasting.
6. Most of the subjects in the sample from the two cities did not attend religious meetings that are presented by religious stations on radio or TV.
7. It was found that most of the respondents from Group A and Group B listened to or watched religious broadcasting on TV on Sundays.
8. The data indicated that the respondents did not for the most part, look or listen to religious broadcasting during the week.
9. The respondents from Long Beach and from Los Angeles — for the most part — said that they did not know of anyone being "saved" by listening to religious broadcasting.
10. Most of the subjects from Group A and Group B stated that they did not know of anyone giving up a bad habit because of listening or watching a religious broadcast.
11. Approximately half of the respondents from Group A and from Group B thought that the people who participate in religious broadcasting are sincere.
12. There was no significance of opinion between the two groups regarding the sincerity of people who participate in making religious broadcasts.

APPENDIX IV

(Facsimile of article as it appeared in Emerging Trends, Vol. 1, No. 5, May 1979, Princeton Research Center, Princeton, New Jersey)

WILL "ELECTRIC CHURCH" REPLACE TRADITIONAL WORSHIP

Religious broadcasting, or the "electric church," as Ben Armstrong of the National Religious Broadcasters describes it, is growing at the rate of approximately one radio station per week and one television station per month. Armstrong, the executive director of the NRB, states that the majority of this growth has been in the last ten years and that US religious broadcasters touch the lives of more people than all this country's churches combined.

The NRB alone has grown from 104 stations in 1967 to 850 stations today (both radio and TV) — and the introduction of cable and satellites suggests a much greater expansion in the future.

Findings in a study on the "Unchurched American," conducted by the Gallup Poll, the Princeton Religion Research Center and a coalition of 30 religious groups, indicate that 28% of the unchurched have listened to, or watched, radio and TV programs produced by a religious organization in the last 30 days. Six in ten unchurched Americans were not exposed to religious broadcasting in this same time period.

Instead of a substitute for church attendance, the effects of the "electric church", in the view of some, may help increase membership. As a result of watching and listening to a religious program in the past 30 days, 14% of the unchurched consider becoming an active member in a church.

The following tables list the types of programs watched, as well as some of the specific programs themselves.

What kind were they—were they any of these kinds? Read off as many as you saw or heard. Just read off the letters. (Asked of unchurched respondents who have listened to, or watched a religious program in the last 30 days.)

Broadcasts of religious services	55%
Testimonial or Crusade program	32%
Religious talk show	23%
Documentaries about actual people or events	19%
Dramatizations about the Bible	16%
Short spot messages	13%
Special holiday programs	11%
Animated cartoons	4%
Other	7
Don't Know/No answer	3%
	**183%

**Total adds to more than one hundred percent due to multiple responses.

Do you remember the names of the programs or the sponsoring groups? What were they? (Asked of unchurched respondents who have listened to, or watched a religious program in the past 30 days.)

Oral Roberts	12%
Billy Graham	11%
Rex Humbard	4%
P.T.L.	3%
Sponsored by the Baptists	3%
700 Club	3%
Dr. Robert Schuller	3%
Lutheran Church sponsors	1%
Garner Ted Armstrong	1%
Larry Black	1%
Holocaust	1%
Only gave call numbers	2%
Other	19%
Don't Know/No answer	53%
	**117%

**Total adds to more than one hundred percent due to multiple responses.

APPENDIX V

(Facsimile of article as it appeared in Central States Speech Journal, Spring 1959)

A TELEPHONE SURVEY OF RELIGIOUS PROGRAM PREFERENCES AMONG LISTENERS AND VIEWERS IN LOS ANGELES
by
Fred L. Casmir
Pepperdine College

This study attempts to supply an answer to a question often asked by religious speakers and laymen alike: How effective are religious radio and television programs in reaching people who do not usually attend religious services? The information gained by this study represents an important means in determining the value of present day programs of a religious nature — as far as the reactions of people living in the Los Angeles area are concerned.

I. INTRODUCTION

The writer, who is a minister, is interested in the question of the effectiveness of religious broadcasting. The type of "sponsor-studies" done in commercial radio and television have been used only to a very limited extent to determine the effectiveness of religious radio and television programs. By "effectiveness" this writer means the ability of a given religious program to reach people who would otherwise not be reached by religious groups. One cannot apply the same standards to religious programs which are used for commercial programs, their basic aims are much too different. However, it is not necessary to close one's eyes to the fact that there are ways of appraising the success or failure of religious programs.

How little information is available to the student of religious radio and television, especially as far as the audiences of these media is concerned, can be illustrated by the fact that a bibliography developed by Gertrude G. Broderick in 1956 for the U. S. Department of Health, Education and Welfare lists only one book in this area. This book, "The Television-Radio Audience and Religion" (Everett C. Parker, David W. Barry, Dallas W. Smythe; Harper Brothers, Publishers. New York: 1955), has become somewhat of a "standard" in the area. In the preface, Oscar Katz, Director of Research at C.B.S. Television makes the following statement, which still holds true to a large degree:

> Considering the importance that radio and television have assumed in the American social and cultural scene, it is surprising that up to now no start has been made in describing the place of religious broadcasting in American life and analyzing its effect.

This fact is further illustrated by the absence of references to related studies or reports in the book by Parker, Barry, and Smythe. However, these men provide students of the area with much detailed information on the religious viewing and listening habits of one community, New Haven, Connecticut.

The present study is interested in one phase of religious broadcasting research, namely the relationship of church attendance and viewing/listening habits, in the case of religious programs only. On pages 109 and 110 of the book cited above an interesting statement is made which has an important bearing on the present study:

> The conclusion is evident that most religious programs are conceived of as means whereby a religious in-group can make some contact with the multitude outside the fold. We shall see subsequently (Chapters 10 and 11) that for most of these programs, especially those with smaller audiences, achievement of this purpose is a highly optimistic assumption. The audience is actually composed of the faithful, rather than of potential converts. One is forced to the decision that few of the broadcasters have any clear picture of the audiences which their programs actually reach.

However, a detailed analysis or comparison of viewing/listening habits to church attendance was not carried through. The writer feels that a reexamination of many religious programs should be the result, if we consider carefully some of the data gathered in the study described on the following pages.

II. DEVELOPMENT OF A QUESTIONNAIRE

The writer developed a questionnaire which enabled trained students to obtain pertinent information over the telephone, in a period of from three to four minutes per call. Data concerning listener's and viewer's preferences for religious radio and television programs in the Los Angeles area were thus gathered.

After several "dry-runs" and instruction periods under the supervision of the writer, the students were able to conduct the calls satisfactorily. Using data from the Los Angeles Telephone Company, a proportionate number of telephone numbers from each of the twenty Central exchanges was determined.

Eleven students made 1200 calls, of which 494 resulted in completed questionnaires. All calls were completed during the months of March and April, 1957. Students were instructed to terminate calls immediately if the subjects who were called declined to answer the questions. In case of busy signals, students were instructed to call one of the alternate numbers of the same telephone exchange. One of the first questions asked of the subjects was concerned with their religious faith. Students reported little or no difficulty on this question from those who agreed to cooperate in answering the questionnaire. Only 12 questionnaires had to be discarded because of insufficient data concerning the faith of respondents.

The calls were made during the following periods:

9:30–11:30 a.m. (32.4% of all calls)
1:30–4:30 p.m. (50.9% of all calls)
6:30–7:30 p.m. (16.7% of all calls)

III. VITAL STATISTICS OF THE SAMPLE

The total group of 494 was divided into religious and racial groups as indicated in Table I and Table II.

TABLE I
RELIGIOUS FAITHS WITHIN TOTAL SAMPLE OF 494

Faith	Number	Percentages
Protestants	349	70.6%
Catholic	128	25.8%
Jews	17	3.6%

TABLE II
RACIAL GROUPS WITHIN TOTAL SAMPLE OF 494

Race	Number	Percentages
White	329	66.7%
Negro	110	22.3%
Mexican/Spanish	48	9.6%
Oriental	7	1.4%

Of the total population in Los Angeles, according to the 1954 census figures, 34% were Protestants, 20% were Catholics and 5% were Jews. Furthermore, of the total population in Los Angeles, according to the 1950 Census (Total population being 1,970,358) 93.9% were White (Mexicans included), 4.2% were Negro, and 1.9% were Oriental.

Of the total groups of 494, (100%) 103 were men (21%) and 391 were women (79%).

IV. EVALUATION OF THE STUDY SAMPLE

A considerably larger percentage of the subjects were women (79%) while men made up 21% of the total.

All racial groups were represented in somewhat the same order as they compose the Los Angeles population, although they were not represented by the same percentages as in the total population.

The size of the sample, 494 subjects, taken from such a varied group, should be sufficiently large to indicate existing trends, the Jewish group of 17 subjects, however, is probably too small to permit the drawing of any reliable conclusions on data secured from this group alone.

V. LISTENER PREFERENCES

Only those subjects who had access to both radio and television sets were included in the sample of 494.

A: First it was determined which broadcasting medium, radio or television, subjects of this study preferred for religious programs.

TABLE III
PREFERENCE FOR BROADCASTING MEDIA

Faith	Radio Preferred	TV Preferred	No Preference
349 Protestants	(131) 37.6%	(179) 51.3%	(39) 11.1%
128 Catholics	(58) 45.4%	(8) 6.2%	(62) 48.4%
17 Jews	(5) 29.4%	(8) 47.1%	(4) 23.5%
Total: 494	(194) 39.3%	(195) 39.5%	(105) 21.2%

Results:

The total group was almost equally divided as to its preferences of radio or television (39%). 21.2% had no preference. More Catholics preferred radio than any other group (45.4%). Protestants (51.3%), and Jews (47.1%) preferred television over radio.

B: Secondly it was determined how many people both listened to religious programs on radio, and watched them on television.

TABLE IV
NUMBER OF PEOPLE LISTENING TO RADIO AND
VIEWING TELEVISION FOR RELIGIOUS PROGRAMS

Faith	Radio and Television
349 Protestants	(164) 46.7%
128 Catholics	(56) 43.5%
17 Jews	(11) 64.7%
Total: 494	(231) 47.0%

Results:

These data indicate that almost half of the subjects of this study avail themselves of religious programs both on radio and television (47.5%). For the Jewish group, 64.7% both listen to religious programs on radio and view them on television.

C: Thirdly, the average time spent listening to and viewing reli-

134

gious programs each week was determined.

TABLE V
AVERAGE TIME SPENT IN LISTENING AND VIEWING
RELIGIOUS PROGRAMS

Faith	Average Time	(Hours and Minutes)	
Protestants	2 hours	14	minutes
Catholic	1 hour	28	minutes
Jews	1 hour	4	minutes

Results:

Combining all three faiths, an estimated average of 1 hour and 48 minutes, of both listening to and viewing of religious programs is done by the subjects of this study. Protestants included in this group did the greatest amount of listening and viewing: 2 hours 14 minutes (average per week).

D: Fourth, the listener's and viewer's preferences as to days for religious broadcasts, was determined.

TABLE VI
PROTESTANTS' PREFERENCES OF DAYS FOR
RELIGIOUS BROADCASTS

Monday	Tuesday	Wednesday	Thursday	Friday	Saturday	Sunday	Any Day
(27)	(17)	(16)	(14)	(19)	(17)	(163)	(76)
7.7%	4.9%	4.6%	4%	5.4%	4.9%	46.8%	21.7%

TABLE VII
CATHOLICS' PREFERENCES OF DAYS FOR
RELIGIOUS BROADCASTS

Monday	Tuesday,	Wednesday	Thursday	Friday	Saturday	Sunday	Any Day
(8)	(6)	(6)	(7)	(5)	(9)	(61)	(26)
6.3%	4.7%	4.7%	5.4%	3.9%	7.1%	47.3%	20.4%

TABLE VIII
JEWS' PREFERENCES OF DAYS FOR
RELIGIOUS BROADCASTS

Monday	Tuesday	Wednesday	Thursday	Friday	Saturday	Sunday	Any Day
(1)	(1)	(0)	(0)	(2)	(0)	(9)	(4)
5.9%	5.9%			11.8%		52.9%	23.5%

Results:

The greatest number of Protestants preferring a day was 163, the day Sunday. However, each one of the weekdays was chosen by some Protestants, 76 had no preference as to any specific day of the week on which to listen to or view religious programs. (Table VI)

Catholic preferences as to days were very similar to those of the Protestant group. Sunday was the day most preferred. (Table VII)

The general pattern of preferences, observed in the case of both Catholics and Protestants also held true for the Jews. Sunday was the day most preferred. (Table VIII)

E: Fifth, an attempt was made to determine why people listen to religious programs and view them on television. Table IX shows answers given in response to a multiple choice question.

To members of all three faiths the speaker and the subject are most important, with the subject taking the lead for all three faiths. Interesting

136

TABLE IX
REASONS FOR LISTENING AND VIEWING RELIGIOUS PROGRAMS

Reasons	349 Protestants	128 Catholics	17 Jews
Because of the speaker	(107) 30.7%	(49) 38.2%	(6) 35.2%
Because of the subject	(149) 42.7%	(60) 46.9%	(7) 41.2%
Because of the music	(60) 17.2%	(11) 8.6%	(2) 11.8%
Other answers	(33) 9.4%	(8) 6.3%	(2) 11.8%

additional comments can be found in the following list of reasons given under the heading: "Others."

1.   Protestant:
     raised religiously   decent program   recommended
     habit   inclination   try to be good   attention to father
     philosophy   comparison of prophesies   same as going to church
     all should have time for the Lord   like it (3)   my wife listens
     my duty to learn   try to learn what others believe
     to get education of religious nature   just feel religious
     good for subject matter   for entire program   my own church
     no particular reason   Bread of Life   when I feel like it
     dramatic presentation   get a lot out of it   start day off
     variety of ministers   common sense   spiritual

2.   Catholic:
     habit   just like it   all   different each time
     interested in it   want to watch it   no particular reason
     because it's Sunday and I think I ought to

3.   Jewish:
     all 3   varies   depends on program

     F: Somewhat related to the last point was the next question, which was intended to determine if people would rather listen to a speaker of their own faith or to a speaker of another faith (Table X).

137

TABLE X
PREFERENCES FOR RELIGIOUS SPEAKERS

Faith of Listeners	Same Faith	Other Faith	No Preference
349 Protestants	(113) 32.5%	(20) 5.7%	(216) 61.8%
128 Catholics	(58) 45.2%	(9) 7.3%	(61) 47.5%
17 Jews	(6) 35.4%	0	(11) 64.6%
Total: 494	(177) 35.8%	(29) 5.9%	(288) 58.3%

Results:

A large number of people, 288, had no preferences when it came to the faith of the speaker. In conjunction with the preceding data this seems to indicate that the speaker as a person, and his subject, are most important to these listeners and viewers. Only 29, most Protestants, declared that they would rather listen to a speaker of another faith. Approximately one-third of the Protestant and Jewish subjects preferred speakers of their own faith.

G: The final question is perhaps the most important: Who listens to and/or views religious programs on radio and television? (Table XI)

1.   Catholics made up the largest group attending church regularly with 72.7%; Protestants 54.6%; Jews 23.5%.

2.   Jews made up the largest group attending services seldom with 70.6%; Protestants 31.1%; Catholics 21.1%.

3.   Of those who never attend church, Protestants were the largest group with 14.4%; Catholics 6.2%; Jews 5.9%.

4.   The largest group listening to religious programs on radio were those who listen sometimes (35.6%), while 24.2% listen regularly, and almost the same percentage never listen to religious programs on radio (24.3%).

5.   Figures in TABLE XI indicate that a greater percentage of Protestants from among those who attend church regularly (Total: 191) listen to religious programs on radio either regularly, sometimes, or seldom, than from among those who attend church seldom (Total: 109), or those who never attend church (Total: 49), in that order.

Of regular attendants 91% listen regularly, sometimes, seldom.

Of those who attend seldom 79.8% listen regularly,

TABLE XI
CHURCH ATTENDANCE AND RADIO LISTENING

Faith	Listen Regularly	Listen Some	Listen Seldom	Never	Total
Regular Church Goers					
Protestant	(60) 31.4%	(91) 47.7%	(21) 11.0%	(9) 9%	(191)
Catholic	(12) 12.9%	(23) 24.7%	(16) 17.2%	(42) 45.2%	(93)
Jewish	0	(2) 50.0%	(2) 50.0%	0	(4)
Occasional Church Goers					
Protestant	(26) 23.9%	(37) 33.9%	(24) 22.0%	(22) 20.2%	(109)
Catholic	(10) 37.1%	(6) 22.2%	(3) 11.1%	(8) 29.6%	(27)
Jewish	0	(5) 41.7%	(3) 25.0%	(4) 33.3%	(12
Non-Church Goers					
Protestant	(11) 22.5%	(8) 16.3%	(10) 20.4%	(20) 40.8%	(49)
Catholic	0	(3) 37.5%	0	(5) 62.5%	(8)
Jewish	0	(1) 100%	0	0	(1)
TOTALS					
349 Protestants	(97) 27.8%	(136) 38.9%	(55) 15.8%	(61) 17.5%	
128 Catholics	(22) 17.2%	(32) 25.0%	(19) 14.8%	(55) 43.0%	
17 Jews	0	(8) 47.1%	(5) 29.4%	(4) 23.5%	
TOTALS: 494	(119) 24.2%	(176) 35.6%	(79) 15.9%	(120) 24.3%	

sometimes, seldom.

Those who attend never have 59.2% listening regularly, sometimes, seldom.

6. Figures in TABLE XI indicate that Catholics who seldom attended church listened most to religious radio programs. Catholics who never attended church listened least.

Of regular attendants 54.8% listen regularly, sometimes, seldom.

Of those who attend seldom 70.4% listen regularly, sometimes, seldom.

Those who attend never have 37.5% listening regularly,

sometimes, seldom.

7. Figures in TABLE XI indicate that of those Jews who never attend services 100% listen to religious programs sometimes. In the case of Jews who regularly attend services 100% either listen to religious programs sometimes or seldom. This figure represents eight Jews. 66.7% of the Jews seldom attending services listen to religious programs on radio either sometimes or seldom, this group also includes eight Jews. It is interesting to note that none of the Jewish respondents reported regular listening to religious radio programs.

8. The largest percentage of regular radio listeners for Protestants came from among those who attend church regularly (31.4%), for Catholics from those who attend church seldom (37.1%).

Results:

(Data on church attendance are included as points 1, 2, 3, among the radio-listening results.)

1. Considering the viewing habits of the total group, the largest percentage was the group which sees religious programs sometimes, 31.2%, whild 26.1% watch regularly, and 20.3% never watch religious programs on television.

2. Figures in TABLE XII indicate that a greater percentage of Protestants from among those who attend church regularly (Total: 191) view religious programs on television either regularly, sometimes, or seldom, than from among those who never attend church (Total: 49) or those who attend church seldom (Total: 109), in that order.

Of regular attendants 84.8% view regularly, sometimes, seldom.

Of those who attend seldom 75.2% view regularly, sometimes, seldom.

Of those who attend never 77.6% view regularly, sometimes, seldom.

3. Figures in TABLE XII indicate that a greater percentage of Catholics from among those who attend church regularly (Total: 93) view religious programs on television either regularly, sometimes, or seldom, than from among those who never attend church (Total: 8) or those who attend church seldom (Total: 27) in that order.

Of regular attendants 76.3% view regularly, sometimes, seldom.

Of those who attend seldom 71.4% view regularly, sometimes, seldom.

TABLE XII
CHURCH ATTENDANCE AND TV VIEWING

Faith	Listen Regularly	Listen Some	Listen Seldom	Never	Total
		Regular Church Goers			
Protestant	(61) 31.9%	(67) 35.1%	(34) 17.8%	(29) 15.2%	(191)
Catholic	(26) 28.0%	(29) 31.1%	(16) 17.2%	(22) 22.7%	(93)
Jewish	0	(1) 25.0%	(2) 50.0%	(1) 25.0%	(4)
		Occasional Church Goers			
Protestant	(21) 19.2%	(35) 32.1%	(26) 23.9%	(27) 24.8%	(109)
Catholic	(9) 33.3%	(6) 22.3%	(4) 14.8%	(8) 29.6%	(27)
Jewish	(3) 25.0%	(1) 8.3%	(8) 66.7%	0	(12)
		Non-Church Goers			
Protestant	(7) 14.3%	(12) 24.5%	(19) 38.8%	(11) 22.4%	(49)
Catholic	(2) 12.5%	(3) 37.5%	(2) 25.0%	(2) 25.0%	(8)
Jewish	(1) 100%	0	0	0	(1)
		TOTALS			
349 Protestants	(89) 25.5%	(114) 23.7%	(79) 22.6%	(67) 19.2%	
128 Catholics	(36) 28.1%	(38) 29.7%	(22) 17.2%	(32) 25.0%	
17 Jews	(4) 23.5%	(2) 11.8%	(10) 58.8%	(1) 5.9%	
TOTALS: 494	(129) 26.1%	(154) 31.2%	(111) 22.4%	(100) 20.3%	

Of those who attend never 75.0% view regularly, sometimes, seldom.

Approximately the same percentage of people is being reached by religious television broadcasts in each Catholic attendance group.

4. Figures in TABLE XII indicate that of those Jews who never attend services, 100% view religious programs regularly, however, only one Jew is here represented by the 100%. In the case of the Jews who attend services seldom, 100% of the group (involving 12 Jews) viewed religious programs either regularly, sometimes, or seldom. 75.0%, or four Jews, who attend services regularly viewed religious programs either sometimes or seldom.

5.   The largest percent of regular television viewers for Protestants came from among those attending church regularly (31.9%), for Catholics from among those who attend church seldom (33.3%), and for Jews from among those who never attend services (1 Jew or 100%).

Conclusions

The author would like to quote portions of the conclusions drawn by Parker, Barry and Smythe, since these statements are further borne out by the present study:

> Perhaps the most persistent error on the part of religious broadcasters, an error that appears constantly in statements and literature, is the assumption that because the media are almost universal, they therefore deliver to any program an audience representative of universality. It is fair to say, on the basis of the evidence presented, that the clergyman who presents on the air a duplication of what he presents from the pulpit will have as his audience about the same group as those who will come to church to hear him . . . the audience even in numerical terms in a town such as New Haven does not seem to be larger than a fair-sized Sunday morning congregation.[1]

Both the selection of religious speakers and program types should be carefully considered on the basis of findings discussed in this study.

[1]Parker, Everett C., Barry, David W., Smythe, Dallas W., *The Television-Radio Audience and Religion.* Harper & Brothers, Publishers, New York. 1955.

CHAPTER FOOTNOTES

Chapter I

[1]Kane, Joseph, *Famous First*, Third Edition, NY: The H. W. Wilson Co., 1964, p. 408.

[2]Plowman, Edward, "Carter's Presence Confirms Clout of Evengelical Broadcasters," *Christianity Today*, Feb. 22, 1980, p. 49.

[3]Kane, op.cit., p. 605.

[4]Plowman, op.cit., p. 48.

[5]"Stars of the Cathode Church," *Time*, Feb. 4, 1980, p. 65.

[6]Kane, op.cit., p. 609.

[7]Wynn, Lawson, "The Next Stage in Satellite Communications," *Religious Broadcasting*, June/July 1978, p. 17.

[8]Megill, Virgil, "The Origins of NRB," *Religious Broadcasting*, February/March 1977, p. 35.

[9]Bleum, James, *Religious Television Programs*, NY, p. 205.

Chapters II and III

*Reprinted—Gospel Radio by Barry Siedell, The Good News Broadcasting Association, Lincoln, Nebraska, 1971.

Chapter IV

[1] "KNX Observes Golden Anniversary," KNX news release, Sept. 1970, p. 1.

[2] Ibid., p. 2.

[3] "KPPC: December 25, 1924," *Religious Broadcasting*, February 1977, p. 30.

[4] "Dr. Eugene Scott and Faith Center Church," KHOF news release, n.d.

[5] Herbeck, Ray, "2 'Born Again' Outlets due for LA Audience Battles," *Billboard*, August 19, 1978.

[6] Ibid.

[7] "KYMS-Flagship of a New Movement," *Contemporary Christian Music*, June 1979, p. 1.

[8] "Religious Broadcasting—Big, Big Business," *MAC-Media Agencies Clients*, February 12, 1979, p. 1.

[9] Ringsburg, Jeff, "Inspirational Radio Hits LA," *Los Angeles Herald Examiner*, Finance Section, June 12, 1978, p. 1.

[10] Rodney, Les, "KGER Success Story," *Long Beach Independent Press-Telegram*, September 16, 1972, p. B-3.

[11] King, Pamela, "Born Again Media," *Los Angeles Herald Examiner*, January 7, 1978, p. A-7.

[12] "Ecumenical Insights Airs Series Giving Black Perspective on Religion," *Carson Courier*, June 8, 1978, p. 5.; "Women In Religion Series Set," *Los Angeles Herald Examiner*, Feb. 18, 1978, p. A-7.; "Radio Series Begins, *South Bay Daily Breeze*, Feb. 18, 1978, p. A-15.

[13] "Unity Discussed—InterFaith Forum," *Los Angeles Sentinel*, Entertainment Section, October 13, 1977, p. B-2A.

[14]*Baha'i Nightingale Newsletter*, August 1978.

Chapter V

[1]Aversa, Rudy, "Ike: Cash Is His Salvation," *Los Angeles Herald Examiner*, August 24, 1974, p. A-7.

[2]Chandler, Russell, "Rev. Ike: He Blesses the Poor With Cult or Money," *Los Angeles Times*, February 27, 1976, p. 1.

[3]Ibid.

[4]Morris, James, *The Preachers*, NY: St. Martin's Press, 1973, p. 175.

[5]Wilcox, Robert, "Ministry of Love Made Easier by Dollars," *Miami News*, April 1971.

[6]Ibid.

[7]Kinsolving, Lester, "Rev. Ike." *Abilene Reporter-News*, February 26, 1972, p. 4.

[8]Morris, op.cit., p. 179.

[9]Ibid.

[10]Hazard, David, "Freedom to See One Man's Escape from the Blindness of Bigotry," *Christian Life*, July 1979.

[11]Taylor, Brooke, "Ben Kinchlow-An Unlikely Convert," *Newport News Daily Press*, June 11, 1978, p. 3.

[12]Ware, Irene, "Gospel," *Black Radio Exclusive*, 3/15/78, p. 12.

[13]"Singing Pastor Scores Movie Role," *St. Louis Post Dispatch*, September 25, 1978.

[14]"Fellowship's TV Service," *Chicago Defender*, Feb. 25, 1978.

[15]Banks, Lacy, "What A Fellowship Is Something Else," *Direction*, Fall, 1978, p. 61.

[16]Murray, Virgie, "Fred Price: Teaching Ministry Draws Young People," *Los Angeles Sentinel*, June 22, 1978.

[17]Contos, Mike, "WYIS To Go On the Air Tuesday Morning," *Pottstown (PA.) Mercury*, August 18, 1978.

[18]"Gospel Show on WJBK-TV," *Billboard*, January 24, 1970 and "Motor City Gospel on Channel 7," *Detroit News*, January 22, 1970.

[19]Heilbut, Tony, *The Gospel Sound: Good News and Bad Times*, NY: Simon and Schuster, 1971.

[20]"Radio Station at Lorton," *Washington Star*, October 16, 1977.

[21]National Council of Churches Newsletter, March 1, 1970.

[22]Heilbut, op.cit.

[23]*Bilalian News*, October 27, 1978, p. 12.

[24]"It Started On Saturday Nights," *Decision*, June 1978, p. 4.

[25]Jones, Howard, "Evangelize Our Cities Now," *Freedom*, n.d.

[26]"New Station Heads for Big Time," *Religious Broadcasting*, February/March 1979, p. 74.

[27]"WYCB: Soul for the Soul," *Black Enterprise*, Nov. 1978, p. 19.

Chapter VI

[1]Chandler, Russell, "Evangelical TV Show Picks Up Steam," *Los Angeles Times*, July 31, 1976, p. 2.

[2]"Pat Robertson and CBN," *Broadcasting*, March 6, 1978, p. 56.

[3]"Evangelical TV: Decade of the Tube, *Christianity Today*, March 17, 1972, p. 40.

[4]McDowell, Edwin, "Religious Networks Blossom," *New York Times*, Business & Finance Section, July 23, 1978, p. 1.

[5]Martin, William, "Video Evangelism," *Washington Post*, June 4, 1978

[6]Scudder, Nancy, *Christian Contemporary*, Vol. 3, Nov. 3, 1977, and *Broadcasting*, op.cit., p. 57.

[7]"Rock and Religion: The Domain of a Media Minister," *U.S. News & World Report*, Sept. 24, 1979, p. 38.

[8]"Magnitude of God's Plan for CBN Unfolds," *The Flame*, Jan. 1980, p. 6.

[9]Martin, William, "Heavenly Host," *Texas Monthly*, March 1979.

[10]Ibid.

[11]Ibid.

[12]Fisher, Bob, and Don Kader, "KTBN: Fast—Growing Christian Broadcasting Station," *Broadcast Engineering*, March 1979, p. 48.

[13]Barrett, Art, "It's Non-Stop 'Praise the Lord' on TBN Television," *The Register*, March 19, 1978, p. 2.

[14]Ibid.

[15]"5 Years of God's Miracles," Trinity Broadcasting Network, undated booklet.

[16]Ibid.

[17]Barrett, op.cit., p. A-3.

[18]Ibid.

[19]"The Lord's Network," *Newsweek*, March 20, 1978, p.41.

[20]"PTL: Please Toss a Lifesaver," *Christianity Today*, Dec. 15, 1978, p. 41.

[21]"The PTL Story," undated pamphlet, p. 2.

[22]"PTL Club," undated news release and fact sheet, p. 1.

[23]"PTL Club," new release, January 31, 1980, p. 2.

Chapter VIII

[1]Holsendolph, Ernest, "Religious Broadcasts Bring Rising Revenues and Stir Controversy," *New York Times*, Dec. 2, 1979, p. 1.

[2]Ibid.

[3]Chandler, Russell, "The Electronic Church-Big Time Religion," *Los Angeles Times*, February 25, 1980, p. 3.

[4]Holsendolph, op.cit., p. 10.

[5]"Critics, Electric Church Try Two-way Communication," *Christianity Today*, March 7, 1980, p. 66.

[6]Holsendolph, op.cit., p. 10.

[7]Fore, William, "The Electronic Church," *Ministry*, Jan. 1979, p. 4.

[8]Ibid., p. 6.

[9]Ibid., p. 7.

[10]"Decisions ahead on Deregulation," *Christian Century*, 10-5-79.

[11]Holsendolph, op.cit.

[12]Ibid.

INDEX

Abernathy, Ralph, 41
Addison, Martha, 43
Amos N' Andy, 11
Adamson, Jack, 23
Anderson, Reben, 48
Angel Award, 3, 28
Arai, Sam, 60
Armstrong, Ben, 4, 87,88

Babson, Roger, 90, 91
Baha'i Faith, 18, 27, 29
Bands, William, 39
Bakker, Jim, 1, 4, 21, 59, 60
Bakker, Tammy, 1, 60
Barnhouse, Donald Gray, 10
Bennett, Michael, 92
Benny, Jack, 11
Blazer, Phil, 26
Boice, James, 11
Boone, Pat, 60
Borders, William Holmes, 40
Borrego, Gerado, 24, 48
Bostic, Joe, 45
Branch, Ray, 24, 48
Brown, Joseph, 44
Brown, R. R., 7, 12
Buddhist, 18

Calentine, Paul, 85
Calvary Baptist Church, 6
Calvery Episcopal Church, 1

Carnegie, Dale, 34
Carson, Johnny, 21, 58
Casmir, Fred, 64, 82
Chandler, Russell, 87
Christian Broadcasting Network (CBN), 51-56
Christian, Fred, 19
Cleveland, E. E., 48
Cleveland, James, 21
Cobb, Clarence, 44
Coleman, Sam, 40
Coley, John Ford, 29
Collins, Ollie, 21, 49
Colson, Chuck, 60
Context, 89
Cosnard, Roland, 60
Couch, Paul, 1, 56-59
Couch, Jan, 1
Craner, Walt, 92
Crawford, Lois, 3,4
Crofts, Dash, 29
Crosby, Bing, 11
Crouch, Andrae, 21
Cunningham, Darby, 21, 49

Dan, England, 29
Daddy Grace, 32
Danibelle, 21
David, Barry, 64
Davis, Jay, 25
Davis, Willie, 40

DeHaan, M. R., 16
Dorr, Mary, 28
Dothery, Frank, 20
Duarte, Charles, 20
Dunlop, Merrill, 14
Dyan, Moshe, 58

Ecumenical Insights, 27, 81
Eldersueld, Peter, 17
Emerging Trends, 64, 83
Epp, Theodord, 11, 16
Erickson, Clarence, 14
Ervin, Jim, 61
Evans, Clay, 30, 36

Farrakhan, Louis, 46
Father Divine, 32
Faust, Rusty, 26
Federal Council of Churches of Christ (FCCC), 2
The Flame, 55
Flower, Clint, 24
Flynn, Tim 57
Fore, William, 4, 87, 88
Fosdick, Harry, 104
Franklin, Aretha, 43
Franklin, C. L., 43
Fuller, Daniel, 9

Gallup, 64, 65, 77
Graham, Billy, 4, 31, 47
Grant, Robert, 39
Gregory, Tenicia, 39
Griffin, Joseph, 40
Gillespie, Dizzy, 29
Gilliam, Stu, 29
Gopaul, Paul, 46

Hackett, Cal, 49
Hardyway, Robert, 24, 48

Harrison, Harry, 59
Hart, B. Sam, 42, 47
Hatfield, Mark, 60
Hawkins, Walter, 21
Hill, George, 64, 79, 82, 116
Hill, John Lamar, 39
Hodges, J. Morgan, 44
Hubbard, David Allen, 9
Hubbard, Garfield, 44
Humbart, Maude Aimee, 1
Humbart, Rex, 1, 4

Idahosa, Benson, 59
Interreligious Council of Southern California (IRC), 18
InterFaith Forum, 27, 81
Ike, Rev., 30-34
Islam, 18
Islam, Nation of, 46, 49

Jackson, Mahalia, 36, 44
Jerigan, Eddie, 48
Jewish, 18, 26, 27, 63, 69, 72, 82, 103
John, Elton, 29
Johnstone, Ronald, 64, 67, 82, 107
Jones, Clarence, 5, 12
Jones, Dean, 60
Jones, Howard, 47
Jones, Wanda, 47
Jones, William A., 45

Kilgore, Thomas, Jr., 40
Killman, Russell, 14
Kinchlow, Ben, 30, 34, 47
King, A. D., 41
King, Corretta Scott, 41
King, Martin Luther, Jr., 41, 46, 48
King, Martin Luther, Sr., 41
Knight, Gladys and The Pips, 29

Kollek, Teddy, 58
Kolman, Kenneth, 31

Larson, Reuben, 12
LeSea Broadcasting, 61
Lewis, David, 60
Liebert, Robert, 86, 87
Literary Digest, 89, 90
Lubin, Ed, 23
Lutheran Hour, 12, 107

McCardell, A. A., 42
McFarlind, Catherine, 48
McGee, Parker, 29
MacKenzie, Beth, 29
McMahon, Ed, 59
McMillian, Carl, 56
McPherson, Aimee Simple, 19, 33, 126
McClatchey, Arnie, 22
Maier, Walter, 4, 12
Malcolm X, 35, 46
Martin, Marty, 54, 87, 89
Martin, Sally, 44
Martin, William, 54
Massey, James, 43
Mays, Joe, 36
Menitoff, Mike, 26
Meyer, Paul, 14
Ministry, 89
Mitchell, Henry, 45
Moody Bible Institute, 10
Muhammad, Elijah, 46, 49
Muhammad, Wallace Dean, 46

National Christian Network, 63
National Council of Churches (NCC), 4, 45, 86
National Religious Broadcasters Association, 4, 42, 87

Nelson, Dorothy, 29
Nicholas, Fayard, 29

Parker, Everette, 4, 64, 72, 76, 81, 85, 83
Paxton, Gary, 60
Peale, Norman Vincent, 1, 34
Pope, Liston, 65
Praise The Lord (PTL) 59-63
Price, Fred, 30, 36

Rader, Paul, 5, 12
Ranger, Blanch, 41
Ranger, R. E., 42
Rayford, M. L., 48
Redbook, 83
Reed, Sarah, 41
Religion In Media Association (RIM), 2, 28
Rev. Ike, 25, 30-34
Reynolds, Jeff, 29
Roberts, Oral, 4, 33
Robinson, Cleopus, 30, 36
Romero, Juan, 59
Roos, John, 87
Roosevelt, Franklin Delano, 9
Robertson, A. Willis, 51
Robertson, Pat, 4, 21, 51-54
Russell, Clayton, 39
Ryan, Quin, 89

Sanders, Howard, 48
Seals, Jimmy, 29
Scott, Gene, 21
Schuller, Robert, 4, 87
Schultze, Harry, 17
Shearer, William "Bill", 40
Sheen, Fulton, 126
Sikh Dharma, 18
Smith, Benjamin, Sr., 42

Smith, Ed, 43
Smith, J. Harold, 14, 15
Smith, J. T., 48
Smythe, Dallas, 64
Straton, John Roach, 6
Sumrall, Lester, 63

Taylor, Gardner, 45
Thomas, Eugene, 40
Thorpe, Rosetta, 36
Trinity Broadcasting Network, 56-59

VanEtten, Edwin, 1
Vedanta Society, 18
Vorspan, Max, 26

Walker, Wyatt, 46
Ware, Irene Johnson, 41
Webb, T. Myron, 11
Whiteman, Fred, 25
Williams, Eric, 13
Williams, Samuel, 47
Williams, Smallwood, 44, 47
Wilson, Ernie, 43
Wings Over Jordon, 76, 104
Wolfe, O. O., 48
Wonder, Stevie, 29, 39
Wynn, Ed, 11

Year of Sunday, 29

Zoller, John, 15